"People throughout history have been fascinated and attracted by a well-told story. The biblical story, which focuses on God's dealings with humankind, is the greatest story ever told. In this fresh treatment of the role of storytelling in the communication of the gospel, Christine Dillon, using her extensive personal experience of working crossculturally, writes winsomely and helpfully about ways in which we can engagingly bring the gospel alive through the art of story-telling in a global generation of increasing numbers of oral learners who love to hear a good story. There is no greater story to be told than the story of God's love for people in the person of Jesus Christ. This book will be help you be more effective in telling that story."

Lindsay Brown, former general secretary of IFES and former international director of the Lausanne Movement for World Evangelization

"I appreciate Christine Dillon's knowledge and experience of using storytelling in evangelism. Many people love to talk about 'orality' and theorize on how and why it should work. Christine learned the concepts of storytelling and immediately started using them. Over the years, she has had to improve her skills, change her approach and develop her methods. This ongoing process has been key in her success. Now she has written down what she has learned. This is a must-read for those wanting to develop these same skills."

John Walsh, president, Christian Storytelling Network

"At last, a really practical book on Bible storying! Christine Dillon gives us a step-by-step guide on how to tell Bible stories based on a carefully laid biblical foundation, nuggets of wisdom from her re-search and her own experiences of telling Bible stories on planes, at the hairdresser, with friends and on the streets. The result is a book that encourages, inspires and helps me to use storytelling much more often in sharing the message of the Bible with Muslims. I will be highly recommending it to all my students and Christian friends."

Richard Hibbert, director, School of Cross-Cultural Mission, Sydney Missionary & Bible College

"This is an excellent book that I would encourage all serious Christians to read. Using moving stories, Christine shares insights she has learned about telling (gospel) stories effectively. She answers the questions that will come to the reader's mind. Christine is honest that this method will not cause all to come to Christ, but the method may have the best chance of people hearing the whole story and wanting more. I will be recommending this book for all our workers, both new and experienced."

Richard Schlitt, deputy general director, OMF

"Christine has given us a most welcome introduction and primer in her book *Telling the Gospel Through Story*. While her context is cross-cultural, she makes a strong case for pastors and evangelists everywhere to understand the importance of, and the ways and means to share, biblical narratives. This book will be helpful in all gospel preaching and homiletics in general."

Lon Allison, executive director, Billy Graham Center, Wheaton College, and author, *Going Public with the Gospel*

"We live by stories. Family stories. Celebrities' stories. Historical stories. Something happens. And then—? We stop to listen. We can't help it. The story pulls us in. Much of God's revelation is story. People act, but even before that, God acts. Christine Dillon knows the power of God's never-ending story. In this book she shows us how to tell it so as to transmit truth that will transform the listeners."

Miriam Adeney, author of *Kingdom Without Borders: The Untold Story of Global Christianity*

"Human beings make sense of our lives through stories. Yet all too often when it comes to evangelism, Christians offer some abstract theological propositions for people to agree with or not, rather than inviting them to enter the Story the Bible is narrating. Christine Dillon calls us to recapture the beauty, power and mystery of storying the gospel, and does so with the wisdom of a practitioner."

Sean Gladding, author of *The Story of God, the Story of Us*

TELLING
THE GOSPEL
THROUGH STORY

Evangelism That Keeps Hearers Wanting More

Christine Dillon

IVP Books

An imprint of InterVarsity Press
Downers Grove, Illinois

InterVarsity Press
P.O. Box 1400, Downers Grove, IL 60515-1426
World Wide Web: www.ivpress.com
E-mail: email@ivpress.com

InterVarsity Press® is the book-publishing division of InterVarsity Christian Fellowship/USA®, a movement of students and faculty active on campus at hundreds of universities, colleges and schools of nursing in the United States of America, and a member movement of the International Fellowship of Evangelical Students. For information about local and regional activities, write Public Relations Dept., InterVarsity Christian Fellowship/USA, 6400 Schroeder Rd., P.O. Box 7895, Madison, WI 53707-7895, or visit the IVCF website at <www.intervarsity.org>.

Cover design: Cindy Kiple
Interior design: Beth Hagenberg
Images: Stocktrek Images/Getty Images

ISBN 978-0-8308-3794-6

Printed in the United States of America ∞

Library of Congress Cataloging-in-Publication Data

Dillon, Christine.
 Telling the gospel through story: evangelism that keeps hearers wanting more / Christine Dillon.
  p. cm.
 Includes bibliographical references.
 ISBN 978-0-8308-3794-6 (pbk.: alk. paper)
 1. Evangelistic work. 2. Storytelling—Religious aspects—Christianity. I. Title.
 BV3793.D47 2012
 268'.67—dc23

                                                              2012009664

| P | 18 | 17 | 16 | 15 | 14 | 13 | 12 | 11 | 10 | 9 | 8 | 7 | 6 | 5 | 4 | 3 | 2 | 1 |
| Y | 27 | 26 | 25 | 24 | 23 | 22 | 21 | 20 | 19 | 18 | 17 | 16 | 15 | 14 | 13 | 12 |

With all my thanks and praise to him who is the originator, subject and endpoint of the whole of the greatest story of them all. The Holy Spirit has led me, taught me and given me the resources, and I'm so grateful to have been allowed to be a coworker.

For my parents, Bryan and Judy, who first introduced me to the greatest story of them all. I wanted to join you as part of it. Thank you for encouraging me to be all that God made me to be.

And for the staff of Chefoo School in Malaysia, who also taught me the story from when I was five years old. You were indeed some of the hundred parents I was promised in Matthew 19:29 as we left our families for the sake of the gospel. Thank you for introducing me to good stories but most of all for loving me enough to tell me the story I most needed to hear.

CONTENTS

PART FIVE
Adapting for Specific Contexts

INTRODUCTION
The Power of Story

Steve was a house painter from England vacationing at a beach in the Philippines with his family. I happened to be staying at the same resort. One day during a conversation that began to turn toward spiritual things, Steve said, "I've talked to numerous religious leaders but they've never been able to answer my questions satisfactorily. So I've given up on religion and am trying to live a good life."

"What were your questions?" I asked.

"The main one is, why the world is so unfair? Why is there pain and suffering and why doesn't God, if there is a God, do something about it?"

"Could I have a go at sharing something I've learned about these things using a story from the Bible?" I asked.

"I don't believe the Bible."

"That's no problem. I hope you'll find the story helpful anyway."

We started with Genesis 1 and God's intentions for his world. The story concluded, ". . . Then God said, 'Let us make people in our image. He made a man out of the dust of the earth and God breathed his spirit into the man. So Adam became a living being.

Later God put Adam to sleep and took one of his ribs and made a wife, Eve, for him. God said, 'Rule over the animals, . . . multiply and fill the earth.' Finally God looked at everything he had made and blessed it. He said, 'It is very good.' On the seventh day God rested from his work because he had completed the work of creation."

Soon Steve's two children and his son's girlfriend casually drifted over to listen. I filled them in on the story so far and continued by explaining the beginning of pain and trouble in the world from Genesis 3. I mentioned the story's strange hint of hope when God says to Adam and Eve, "The snake and the descendants of the woman will be at war. The snake will strike her descendant's heel, but one day a descendent will crush the head of the snake."

During the discussion one of my listeners said, "I know you're going to say that Jesus is the one coming to crush the snake's head, but how will he do it?"

"Can I tell you a few more stories before Jesus?" I replied. "That will make everything clearer."

So we continued on through the stories of Abraham, the exodus and the rest of the Old Testament. Each story set up the one that followed it so my audience would understand the nature of the human problem and how desperately we needed a Savior. My listeners peppered me with questions, and we discussed them one by one. Most often I asked them a question in return, and they found themselves answering their own questions based on what they'd already learned. Sometimes I said, "That will be answered in an upcoming story."

Finally, after about an hour, we reached the end of the Old Testament. "Come on," they begged. "Don't leave us in suspense. Tell us how Jesus saves!"

Outside our open-air dining room, the beach beckoned. It was a perfect day for snorkeling, and this family had come from winterbound England to play in the sun. Their holiday was almost finished—but today the beach might as well not have existed.

We continued through Jesus' birth and ministry. Finally we reached his death and resurrection. "Do you remember what the temple curtain in the Old Testament symbolized?" I asked.

"The separation between God and people," said one.

"What was the only way people could be forgiven and continue to be friends with God?"

"A representative had to prepare himself carefully and then kill a perfect sacrifice and take its blood through the curtain," another responded.

"So what did it mean when the temple curtain split from top to bottom just when Jesus died?"

They started hesitantly, saying, "I guess it means . . . that because Jesus died . . . the barrier between us and God has been dealt with." Then they concluded in a rush, "So we can once again be friends with God."

"So Jesus was like that perfect sacrifice," one said.

"Yes, but he was also the representative," chimed in another.

At last I called an end to the storying before we'd exhausted ourselves and lost the joy of discovery. Two days later as the family was departing, Steve said, "I'm going home to find my Bible. If those religious experts had told me such relevant stories, I would have happily gone to their church and wouldn't have given up searching."

How did I get involved with Bible storying? I was a reluctant starter. As a teenager, the child of missionaries, I had heard about chronological Bible storying. My impression was that it was best suited for illiterate tribal peoples. When I became a missionary myself, my context was different. I did church planting with OMF International among working-class people in modern, industrialized southern Taiwan.[1] Nearly everyone could read, although a large portion of the population chose to learn in ways other than via the printed word.

I taught the Bible in a wide range of situations, from one-to-one evangelism and discipling to Bible study groups, training seminars and public teaching. I used many stories to illustrate my teaching. Constant feedback and self-evaluation helped improve my teaching, but I never thought to change my basic communication building blocks.

God obviously had a different plan! In 2004 I observed a six-hour OMF training seminar in which the leader told stories from Genesis to the ascension. I enjoyed the stories personally, but I still didn't think they suited my style. I was already a reasonable communicator and believed it would be a huge challenge to adapt my teaching style. Simply put, change of this magnitude seemed like too much work.

So I learned to tell the creation story with reluctance. The next step was to find someone who would listen to it. I chose a busy photo-developing shop for my first attempt—a decision that, looking back, may not have been wise. I didn't do a particularly good job with the story. And a constant flow of customers meant numerous interruptions.

What astounded me was the response of the hearer. She loved the story and wanted to hear more. Suddenly I was no longer having to initiate gospel conversations. Instead people were asking me to tell them about the Bible. The adventure of a lifetime had started.

The wonderful thing about storying is that it's far more than a quick telling of the good news. We Christians often want our evangelistic methods to be time-efficient and produce guaranteed results. But evangelism should not be hurried. People who have heard and discussed many stories come to Christ more prepared than those who are evangelized in other ways. In one sense, you could say that storying is "discipling people to conversion."

If you're reading this book, then you're probably already committed to communicating the gospel in the best way possible. You long to see Jesus glorified, with your family, friends and neighbors part of that crowd rejoicing around the throne (Rev 7:10, 12). Learning to story is worth the investment in time and energy.

I often see hope dawning on people's faces as they're trained in this method. They're delighted to discover that they've found a simple, biblical tool almost anyone can learn.

If you've been frustrated that people don't seem interested in hearing the gospel, this book is for you. I have been amazed at how well storying works. I've found it to be more fruitful and effective than many other approaches to evangelism. It's a natural, appealing way to communicate the gospel, and once you get started, people actually want to hear more. Storying has great potential to help many people come to know God, and I am glad to have you join me on this journey. Read on!

PART ONE

FOUNDATIONS

WHY STORYING?

When I think back on the many conversations I've had about the gospel over the years, I often regret that I hadn't known about storying for all of them. For example, many years ago during a holiday in Malaysia, two Christian friends and I ended up on an almost deserted island. It was the month of Ramadan, and the heat combined with the tradition of fasting between sunrise and sunset ensured that the four young men looking after us had little energy. What they did was sit around and talk about religion. Soon they began asking us our opinions. We talked with them for more than an hour each day. I did share some of the exodus story, but I don't remember any more of the conversation. Although God can work through other styles of evangelism, the discussions would have been much richer if storying had been involved.

At the Cape Town 2010 Lausanne Congress, many people observed that poor Bible teaching and discipleship result in a lack of transformation in people's thinking.[1] Weak evangelism is also part of the problem. There can be an unbiblical push for decisions before listeners have understood enough of the gospel, with the result that they don't come to new life. Instead they merely add a layer of superficial thinking on top of their original religious ideas.

There are many effective ways to teach the Bible, including good preaching, evangelistic Bible study and courses that explore Christianity. However, Bible storying is increasingly acknowledged as effective and advantageous. Of course, this method of sharing the gospel is not new. It's as old as the Bible itself. However, since the 1980s there has been a renewed emphasis on using Bible stories as a teaching tool with adults. It seems to have started in crosscultural missions contexts with organizations such as New Tribes Mission and the Southern Baptists' International Mission Board. Using storying in a Western context has been slower to take off. Perhaps missionaries have not realized that it applies in their home contexts, or people have wrongfully dismissed it as a tool for oral learners only.

So if Bible storytelling is such an effective tool, why isn't everyone using it? Well, many don't know about it and have never seen it demonstrated. Most people need to see storying in action before they become enthusiastic about it. And even those who have heard about storying may hold misperceptions that prevent them from getting started.

Misconceptions About Storying

Use the word "story" with people, and they will generally first think of simple children's fairy tales. Stories are often relegated to Sunday school class or bedtime. Kendall Haven, a storyteller and researcher, summarizes this way:

> Stories suffer from a bad reputation—the word tends to be associated with fairy tale, untrue, suspect. . . . You resort to stories if you have a weak case or if you're hiding the truth. . . . Stories have been sidetracked into the kiddy corner and labeled, "just for fun." We believe that story is the opposite of logic, that stories aren't effective for conveying serious and important concepts. And without even consciously pausing to consider either the veracity or implications of

our assumptions, we set aside the most powerful communications and teaching tools available to humans, and then
idly wonder why our efforts to communicate and to teach
concepts, ideas, beliefs, values, attitudes and facts do not
succeed.[2]

In contrast to their reputation, Haven emphasizes that stories
are excellent vehicles for facts.[3] They increase our motivation
and enthusiasm to learn. Without stories, the learning process
can be tedious and dull. Do you remember studying for mathe-
matics, history and science exams? Many of us were taught to
memorize lists of facts, formulas and dates. The concepts were
abstract and disconnected from our lives. How many of these
facts and formulas do you remember now?

Haven tells of a physics teacher who was struggling to help his
class learn what they needed to know. The students simply weren't
interested. So the teacher decided to experiment with storytelling.
For each scientist whose theories he wanted the students to understand, he told stories about the scientist's life and how he or she
came up with the theories. He also painted a picture using stories
of the world they lived in. He was amazed at the difference in his
students. Suddenly they were interested in science and doing well
in the class. Quite a few even went to the library and did extra
research because they'd become so motivated.

Similarly, an international company tried for years to motivate its
salespeople to offer better customer service. The firm used traditional
lecture methods in its training programs but failed to see any results.
Then a speaker told a true story about someone who embodied the
kind of service attitude the company wanted its employees to demonstrate. Now the staff understood. Motivation and enthusiasm levels
changed markedly. Soon the sales force had a number of true stories
to tell at seminars, and employees were competing to show good
service.[4] If the corporate world makes use of stories to train its "evangelists," how much more so should the church?

Stories can help change motivation and values. In addition, stories ensure that information is remembered readily and accurately.[5] Bible stories help hearers to want to be more like Jesus in character, values and priorities, and they help listeners know the truth about him.

A second barrier to getting involved in storytelling is the belief that "it's not my style." This was one of my own objections to getting started, and it's common among seminary graduates and full-time church workers. Bible colleges generally teach abstract, systematic communication styles. But most biblical models use stories and nonabstract styles. (Perhaps this explains why many listeners find our teaching hard to listen to.) Change is difficult. It is especially difficult for those of us who are locked into nonnarrative styles or are already competent using other styles of evangelism and discipleship. Those who most readily embrace storytelling are those who have struggled for years with the model they were given and are desperate to find an evangelism and discipling style that suits them better.

Some introverts may have struggled with any form of evangelism since the word tends to be associated—mistakenly—with extroversion. Storying is one form of evangelism, among many, that can be performed by introverts. It doesn't have to be done in a large group but can be conducted one-to-one or in small groups. It is a relief to know that we don't have to be fantastic public speakers or naturally outgoing to be successful in storytelling.

Another objection to involvement in storytelling is simply, "I can't do this." Many cultures have lost the habit of storytelling. We might still read stories out loud but we seldom tell them. Even in cultures where storytelling is a traditional art, the advent of television and the Internet means that they are rapidly losing this ability as well. A large percentage of storying trainees say, "I'm not good at telling stories." One wonderful thing about stories is that even a poor storyteller can still communicate. The story itself carries the listener along. A poor story is normally better than no story. Thankfully, storytelling is an art in which improvement is possible. Practice can indeed make perfect.

Some people also doubt that adults will listen to the gospel in story form. We might even feel embarrassed to tell a story to an adult. Won't he or she feel insulted by such a simple approach? Won't people laugh or even ridicule us? Surely an adult's attention won't be held by something so simple. Adults need something "deeper," don't they?

Jim is a member of a Bible study group who has not only experienced storying but has also been trained to use it in evangelism. Despite all the accounts he has heard about its effectiveness and a positive experience himself, he still doubts that nonchurched adults will listen to stories. His doubts mean that he refuses to even try. Instead, he either avoids evangelism altogether or tries other methods with which he feels comfortable. His listeners respond with boredom or indifference. Meanwhile, the other members of the group use storying with adults with excellent response.

Will adults listen to stories? In his research, Kendall Haven examined more than a hundred thousand pages of research across fifteen fields. He also collected anecdotal evidence from thousands of educators and businesses. He concluded that everyone loves stories. Not a single piece of evidence contradicted the premise that stories are universally enjoyed.[6] It is true that many of us can learn via abstract propositions presented in lectures, sermons and evangelistic outlines, especially if these methods suit our learning style or if we've been educated in Western methodology.[7] However, many people around the world in non-Western and even within Western countries don't appreciate abstract concepts. They prefer to learn via stories. If we want our hearers to absorb biblical truth, then we need to evangelize and teach in a way they are enthusiastic about. The good news is that storying helps everybody learn, even the highly educated.

Many of our current evangelistic methods assume that listeners already know the biblical stories. That is, we assume they have a background that allows them to understand nonnarrative teaching. If we're trying to explain that Jesus' death was a substitution, the point is considerably clearer when listeners have heard the stories of the Old Testament where an animal died in the place of someone: whether Isaac (Gen 22), the Passover lamb (Ex 11–12) or the animal sacrificed on the Day of Atonement (Lev 16). The mere reference to familiar stories allows the details to flood back into hearers' minds and fill the word "substitution" with meaning.

Don Carson, a professor at Trinity Evangelical Divinity School, points out that most Western evangelistic methods, which are often exported to the non-Western world, are "subsets of systematic theology":

> By this I mean that they tend to ask atemporal questions, and give atemporal answers. . . . There is nothing intrinsically wrong with this pattern, as long as the people to whom it is presented have already bought into the Judeo-Christian heritage. . . . But if you present these atemporal outlines of the gospel to those who know nothing about the Bible's plotline, and who have bought into one form or another of New Age theosophy, how will they hear you? . . . In short, the good news of Jesus Christ is virtually incoherent unless it is securely set into a biblical worldview.[8]

Perhaps fifty years ago in the West, we could have jumped straight to Jesus in our conversations because many adults had been to Sunday school as children. However, these days most people are biblically illiterate. We can't assume that they've heard the stories of Genesis or Exodus. Even if they are familiar with these stories, they've probably never heard them linked together in any coherent way. The result is like a puzzle that's been thrown in the air with the picture on the box discarded. These people have a little piece of yellow, blue or red, but they have no idea what the whole picture is. We haven't built the necessary foundations so they can understand who Jesus is and why he came.

Storying Opens People to the Gospel

Sometimes storying is the only way people are willing to listen to the gospel. They may have built up defensive walls against other evangelistic methods, had bad experiences in the past, or their own religious leaders have warned them against listening to the Bible. I once met a new Christian while shopping in the market. She told me she'd stopped sharing Jesus with her friends because she was hopeless at it. Whenever her friends saw her coming they began to run away. When she explained her method, it was obvious why her friends were running! The method she was trained to use was confrontational, abstract and manipulative, and it made her friends feel like targets.

I asked this woman if I could demonstrate how I shared with others and launched into the first story. Within a minute, one of the friends she'd alienated came over and asked if she could listen in. At the end of the creation story the friend said, "It's just like watching television."

One huge advantage of using stories is simply that the hearer enjoys the story and doesn't feel threatened by it. My friend James works in a country where it is difficult to share the gospel openly. But he has found that storying is not perceived as evangelism. Recently he's been able to share the gospel with Buddhist monks in a monastery. These monks listened to a set of nine stories and loved them—a Bible study or more formal means of evangelism most likely would not have received a minute of their attention. It might even have been met with vigorous protest. In contrast, the stories seemed harmless. This "harmless" approach allowed the monks to participate in storying groups, and the first one just became a believer after listening to weeks of stories and asking many questions.

Daniel Sanchez, J. O. Terry and LaNette W. Thompson, experienced missionaries and storytellers in the Philippines, Panama and West Africa, write, "People learn best in a non-threatening situation, because they can be more open to what is being taught. In a threatening situation, much of the hearer's unconscious energy goes into preparing to defend against the threat. A story presents concepts in a way that hearers do not feel obliged to agree with them. As a result, the new ideas are more likely to be accepted."[9]

This is one reason that storying is also appreciated by postmodern Westerners. Among many features of postmodern thinking is the idea that all religions are the same and that truth is relative. People often react negatively to presentations of what they perceive as dogmatic truth. However, stories seem to be acceptable style of presentation.[10] Rick Richardson, evangelist and associate professor at Wheaton College, writes,

> Stories [are] the only containers big enough to carry truth, because stories convey not just the facts, but also the feelings and nuances of truth. Stories are a bigger and better container for the whole of the truth than propositions, concepts and dogmas. . . . People today tend to distrust logic and truth when it is expressed propositionally and dogmatically. But when our truth is enfleshed in stories, . . . people are interested. . . . We must recover our own stories, and God's Big Story, and connect them to the stories of people we love and are reaching out to.[11]

Storying Can Be Done with Nonseekers

Many evangelistic methods, such as evangelistic sermons or courses that investigate Christianity, can only be done with people who already want to know more about the Bible or are at least comfortable enough to participate. Storying allows us to share the gospel with hearers who are anti-Christian or haven't yet considered that Jesus could be relevant to their lives. The difference can be pictured like this:

The long length of chain represents a person's life. The point at which we come to new life is represented by the cross (sometimes the exact moment is not possible to pinpoint). I show the links to the left as black, representing life before Christ when we walked in darkness and were spiritually dead. The links to the right I show as green, representing our new life and growth in maturity. The links themselves are people or things God uses to bring us closer to himself. These could be a Bible study, an experience of suffering, a friend's love and concern, the words of a song, a dream—the possibilities are endless because God's creativity is limitless. Storying allows us to share with people substantially further to the left.[12]

A few months ago, during a three-hour flight, I had the privilege of sharing an entire set of stories with a man originally from Pakistan. Our conversation started with my asking him why he was traveling to our destination. This led him to reciprocate with, "And what about you?" I explained that I told Bible stories, and he said he'd never read any of the Bible. We talked a little about the Qur'an, and then I offered to tell him the first story in the Bible. At the end of each story he said, "What's next?" I told fourteen story sections in just over an hour. Then I suggested he find a modern version of the Bible so he could read it for himself. I wrote down my suggestions for where he should start. Storying can turn someone like this man into a seeker.

One of the most difficult parts of evangelism is starting a gospel conversation from scratch. My difficulty in this area has largely been overcome since I started storying. When I met the woman in the photo developing shop, it was easy to ask if she would listen to a story. The subsequent visits were also easier because she naturally asked me for the next one in the series. And if someone doesn't ask, we can simply say, "May I tell you the next story in the set?" This is far easier than spending ages praying for a natural opening to start a gospel conversation.

One of the reasons adults like listening to stories is that they can relate to the characters in them. It's amazing that a story about a man, woman or child who lived in a different culture thousands of years ago can communicate powerfully to us. Stories allow us to laugh and suffer with those people. As we feel for Noah building the ark every day while his neighbors laughed, we think about what we'd do under that kind of pressure. This story also prepares the way for discussion about doing the right thing even when others don't. It's a useful story to refer back to when people are counting the cost and fearing the ridicule and anger of family and friends should they choose to follow Jesus. Peter's denial of Jesus is another powerful story that people identify with, asking themselves, "What would I have done if that had been me? What do I think is more important than Jesus?"

Stories also have a participatory dimension. Bible stories are about God and how he relates to us and us to him. As author and trainer of writers worldwide Miriam Adeney puts it, "We are called to participate in the ongoing story."[13] We can make this participation explicit to our hearers by saying something like, "Abraham was promised that his family would be blessed and this blessing would reach the whole world. The stories that follow will tell you how that happened and how the blessings can come to you here." Later on we can add, "You can be part of sharing the story with others."

Stories often linger long after we've ended a conversation with someone and gone our separate ways. A story will "continue [its] dialogue in mind and memory, expanding not only the truth of the Scriptures . . . but also the capacity of our hearts to receive them."[14] An old man in Taiwan expressed it this way while munching meditatively on some peanuts: "These stories are like peanuts; the more you eat, the better they are and the more they satisfy your heart." My friend Lynne also experienced this as she shared a full set of stories with a Muslim girl in her village. The story of Jesus' resurrection was finished just in time for Lynne and her family to go on home assignment for eight months. Soon after Lynne returned to the village, she went to visit her friend. The girl said, "You know how you asked me why the temple curtain ripped when Jesus died and what it meant? Well, I think I know now." She had been thinking about this question for eight months, along with many others she wanted to ask now as well.

Storying Creates Community

Rachel is a young Christian who works in a convenience store, sharing her shift with one other employee at a time. In order to tell her coworkers stories, she has to do it one-to-one, between customers. She has now told stories to four coworkers. She comments, "There's a different atmosphere at work now. I'm not sure what it is. We're sort of becoming friends, or like a family."

Orality and literacy expert Walter Ong says this is a natural result of storytelling. "Oral communication unites people in groups," he writes. "Reading and writing are solitary activities that throw [us] back on [ourselves]. . . . When a [storyteller] is addressing an audience, the members of the audience normally become a unity, with themselves and with the speaker."[15] Haven concurs, asserting that stories provide "a sense of belonging, a personal commitment to the organization, and a feeling of community."[16] Thus people who hear stories together are drawn closer together by a common experience—that is, via the hearing, discussion and application of the stories to their lives. This is highly relevant to us as Bible storytellers. Storying is a natural bridge into church planting. The church is birthed from those who have gathered to hear the stories and then chosen to trust the Jesus of the stories.

In contrast to a sermon, where a listener tends to stand "outside" and "look in" on what the preacher is saying, stories draw people into the heart of the narrative. Without even realizing it, they begin to see the stories as real. Whenever people tell me they don't believe the Bible, I always respond, "That's fine, just listen to the story." They almost never mention their unbelief again. Somewhere along the way, they're drawn into the reality of the Bible. It's been a long time since I've had to use apologetics in response to the request to "prove to me that the Bible is true."

Storying Helps Theological Understanding

Some people tend to divide the Bible into two categories: simple teaching for those who are less mature and harder stuff for the more mature. They often identify the "simple" stuff as the narrative sections of the Bible and the "harder" material as the Old Testament prophets and New Testament letters and book of Revelation. The goal is to get to the "meat" of Romans, which had such a dramatic impact on spiritual giants such as Augustine, Luther and Wesley.

I believe that this "simple" and "deep" distinction is a false dichotomy. There are simple parts of the prophets and letters and difficult parts of many stories. The difference is that the theological meat is often easier to swallow in story form. The Bible is written in an order that allows theological foundations to be laid so that listeners are able to understand more complex truths later.

For example, I know a middle-aged pork seller who suggested to me that if King Belshazzar had repented in the story found in Daniel 5, God would have accepted him. His life might still have ended, but he himself could have gone to heaven for eternity. That is deep theology stated in simple form. This man had begun to grasp the depth of God's grace and forgiveness.

Likewise, once my beach friend Steve and his family members

had received the biblical story background, they were able to comment on such concepts as substitutionary atonement. They could understand that the tearing of the temple curtain had enormous theological significance. They would not have grasped these concepts as easily without the storying.

Storying Changes Worldview

Slower evangelistic methods like storying maximize the possibility of changing someone's worldview. Worldview, according to freedictionary.com, is "the overall perspective from which one sees and interprets the world and a collection of beliefs about life and the universe held by an individual or a group." Storying changes worldview because it works on people over the long term.

Unless we confront the false beliefs our listeners hold, we just add a veneer of church-ianity on top of their life. British missionary David Eastwood says, "When we share the gospel we are concerned with changing people's worldviews. Anything less would not be real Christianity."[17] The deep beliefs God needs to deal with are well-challenged by stories, as biblical scholar and theologian N. T. Wright points out: "Stories are, actually, particularly good at modifying or subverting other stories and their worldviews. Where a head-on attack would certainly fail, the parable hides the wisdom of the serpent behind the innocence of the dove, gaining entrance and favor which can then be used to change assumptions which the hearer would otherwise keep hidden for safety."[18]

Exactly how a story changes someone's worldview is a mystery. The Holy Spirit works more subtly and thoroughly than we ever could. We tend to lack patience and want to see rapid change, which often leads only to surface change. God takes the time to change people from the inside out. Storying is like the building of a magnificent building. It lays a solid foundation so people are prepared to comprehend the message of the cross and resurrection. On that foundation a building can rise, one that honors

God and will endure for a lifetime of fruitful service. Like any magnificent building, slow and steady work produces the longest-lasting results.

Recently my friend Penny contacted me in distress. "I've tried storying and it doesn't work," she said. Upon probing further, I discovered that she'd developed unrealistic expectations. She hoped that storying was the "magic key" to seeing people come to Christ. Penny expected her listeners to hear one story and suddenly repent. I've never experienced that, and few people do. If you're looking for a magic key, storying is not it—and neither is anything else. I talked with Penny about her expectations, and she shared what happened with her storytelling. It became clear that with some simple adjustments to how she introduced the story and the way she told it, there might be better response and interest next time.

Story can change worldview even when we see people only sporadically. A story is considerably easier to remember than a conversation about abstract concepts. It lingers in the mind, working long after we've parted ways with someone. This is particularly helpful in our relationships with people such as hairdressers, shopkeepers and servers at restaurants. My hairdresser hears a story from me once every three months. We've taken more than two years to cover six Old Testament sections and the Christmas story. This slower pace seems to suit my stylist as she absorbs and thinks about each story. She has no problem remembering previous stories, and usually a minute-long review is all she needs before she's ready for the new story. This is great for a couple of reasons. Not only does she remember the stories, but I never have to search for a way to start a gospel conversation. When I sit down in the chair, she knows it's time for the next installment.

The Surprises of Storying

Anyone who starts telling stories notices after a while how much truth "simple" stories have to teach us. I find myself thinking about the Bible far more often than I did in the past. I've wrestled with tough theological and practical issues through stories as I go about my daily life. I've pondered how Elijah, who had the courage to face 850 prophets of Baal and Asherah (I Kings 18:16-46), could the next day be so terrified for his life that he fled Jezebel's threats. After all, this is the same man whom God miraculously protected by arranging for birds to feed him and for a widow's flour and oil containers to keep miraculously refilling each day (I Kings 17). His frailty and failure to trust God in 1 Kings 19 have made me consider how to avoid ending up in the same depressed condition. I have often reminded myself of the fact that I am never alone, that God always has a remnant serving him like the seven thousand of Elijah's day (I Kings 19:14, 18).

With Daniel, I've considered how to bring God glory in an idolatrous environment like Babylon. How can I follow Daniel's example and not steal God's glory in my daily life? Daniel could easily have told the king he was able to identify the king's dream and then interpret it. Instead he said multiple times and in different ways, "No wise man, enchanter, magician or diviner can explain to the king the mystery he has asked about, but there is a God in heaven who reveals mysteries" (Dan 2:27-28). The stories inspire me, challenge me and slip under my defenses in a way that a command such as "trust God" or "don't steal God's glory" fails to do.

John Walsh, an American storyteller, took a storying team to Thailand. Someone had prearranged for the team to share at a Buddhist school. To their disappointment, when they met the principal she said, "No, no! The team can't teach our children. We've changed our mind. I'm sorry to cause you to come all this way for nothing, but last week we had an American pastor speak in our general assembly. He tried to get all of our children to become Christians. We decided right then we didn't want anymore American Christians speaking to our children. I'm sorry. Your team can't come here."

Well, there was no more to be said. So the team sat there and visited politely with the principal, hoping to lessen the tension of the meeting. They discovered that there was no school the next day because it was the king's birthday. The day was called "Father's Day" since the king was considered the nation's father. The students would be absent, but the teachers would still be present at the school. John said, "Would you like me to teach your teachers how to tell stories? I promise I will keep it secular and not talk about Christianity."

The principal said, "Oh, you would do that—even after I've canceled your program?"

John replied, "Yes, I would be honored."

The next day John taught the teachers basic storytelling techniques to improve their skills. The group laughed and had a good time, but they also applied themselves to learning what John was teaching. By the end of the day, they were all friends. The teachers had worked hard, and John admired their dedication to their profession. Then one teacher spoke up. "This is Father's Day," she said. "Tell us a story about a father." Immediately the rest chimed in and begged for "a father story."

John said, "Well, I have a story about a father, but it's a Bible story, and I said I wouldn't—"

The principal interrupted him. "Oh, it's all right to tell us a Bible story," she said. "These are teachers, not children." So John told them about Abraham and how God gave him and Sarah a child in their old age. John then taught the teachers hand gestures to help them remember the story.

After the group was dismissed, the principal pulled John aside. "If I let you teach our children to tell a Bible story, would it be like that one?"

John said, "If you like that story, I'll make sure the team teaches that very story. And I guarantee you we will do nothing but teach the children to tell the story." He went over the exact details of how the classes would go. Every teacher would help with the lesson. They would then send slips home with the children so parents could sign that their child told the story at least twice outside of school.

Over the next three days, the team taught the "birth of Isaac" story to more than a thousand students in grades three through six. Each student went home and told the story at least twice. More than a thousand children and teachers in Chiang Mai, Thailand, experienced a great crosscultural exchange with American Christian storytellers. And more than three thousand people listened to a Bible story they'd never heard before. The school wrote a letter of recommendation about what happened that week. They commended the team on what they'd done, and they encouraged other schools to take advantage of this opportunity if it were ever offered to them.[19]

Reflection

1. What have been your personal reasons for not sharing stories up to this point? What in this chapter helps you?

2. Do you have other objections to storying? How could you test whether those objections are valid?

3. Compare an evangelism method you've used before and consider that method in light of the advantages of storying. Why might you try storying?

4. Where can you use storying? Pray that God would lead you to someone with whom you might start a storying relationship.

LEARNING FROM
BIBLICAL MODELS

Amanda's family members were idol-worshipers and followed the peculiar blend of Taoism and Buddhism that is prevalent in Taiwan. If asked, Amanda might have said she didn't really know what she believed. Mostly she just followed her parents' traditions without questioning. A friend invited Amanda to church. The main part of the service was a talk that was topical in nature. It was extremely abstract, utilizing illustrations to back up the points. Amanda struggled to concentrate. Afterward she couldn't remember what the speaker had said.

As Christians, we often communicate the Bible and its salvation message in the same way it was modeled to us. Usually our preferred mode of evangelism is to make a series of abstract and "logical" (at least to a Western mind) statements. Let's take a step back and ask ourselves how the Bible itself communicates salvation. How do teachers in the Bible teach? Where does the Bible start? What are its emphases? Does it start with a book like Romans?

Interestingly, the Bible begins not with an explanation of salvation but with a story. This story starts at the beginning and goes to the end. It is essentially chronological, at least in its narrative sections. Genesis 1:1 states that God was alone in the universe and then created all life. It finishes in Revelation with the end of this world as we know it, the re-creation of the heavens and earth and the total fulfillment of God's purposes for his kingdom.

Another surprise is the length of the story. There is no rushing to Jesus and the answer to humanity's problem. Rather, books and books of the Old Testament demonstrate how massive our problem is. Israel's history repeatedly demonstrates that even when God directly reveals himself and performs numerous miracles, people's hearts don't necessarily change. In Egypt, the Israelites "groaned in their slavery and cried out. . . . God heard their groaning and he remembered his covenant with Abraham, with Isaac and with Jacob. So God looked on the Israelites and was concerned about them" (Ex 2:23-25). God provided Moses and through him performed ten incredible miracles—changing a whole river system into blood (Ex 7:14-24), destroying crops with hail and locusts (Ex 9:13-10:20), and hiding the sun for seventy-two hours from the Egyptians while providing normal daylight and nighttime for the Israelites (Ex 10:21-29). These miracles should have led to complete trust in God, yet a short time later the Israelites are panicking because the Egyptian army is coming and they can't cross the Red Sea. Surely, having seen the ten plagues, they'd know to simply ask God to rescue them (Ex 13:14–14:31).

Why do we make our way through such a long story in the Bible before we reach Jesus? Why not go straight from the failure of Adam and Eve in the Garden of Eden to Jesus? After many years of pondering this, I've come to believe that the Old Testament history and the stories of repeated failure are essential for us to be familiar with. First, the Israelites had to come to the point where it was obvious they could never save themselves by "being good" and trying hard to improve. That lesson takes centuries to learn. However, we need that history today too. We need the stories of how the Israelites failed to trust God in many different ways because we need to recognize ourselves in their failures. It is tempting for us to think they were fools and we would have trusted God more readily. Really? We have one huge advantage they didn't: the Bible and the ability to read it. Don't we still regularly worry and fear and forget to trust God? The length of the story of people's failures emphasizes that only a new heart and new life from God will ever change our rebellious nature. There is no other way. The lengthy story prepares us for the relief and joy of God's grace in Jesus.

About two-thirds of the Bible is preparation for Jesus. But we have a tendency to jump straight to proclaiming him. After all, we know that Jesus is the most important. Jesus is indeed the central point of the Bible and, indeed, all of history. The problem is that when we go straight to Jesus, most people's hearts aren't prepared. We want to proclaim, "Jesus is the answer," but many people are still asking, "What's the question?" It's no use telling people the solution to their problem if they are unaware that they have a problem. When God ensured that the Bible was written down, he took his time reaching Jesus.

An experienced missionary and retired Anglican bishop recently pointed out to me that if we don't start with Genesis and who God is, most Asians (and many other people as well) will simply tack Jesus on to their pantheon of gods. He becomes one among many gods. All we end up doing with our "evangelism" is creating syncretists! Starting where the Bible does enables our listeners to grow slowly in their understanding of sin and God's character, especially concerning his holiness and judgment. Lacking these concepts, most people fail to see their need for a Savior. Listeners need adequate Old Testament background to understand the serious nature of humanity's rebellion against God and its consequences. It is also important to learn how people were made right with God in the Old Testament—through a mediator and the blood sacrifice of an innocent animal. This background prepares people to understand the rich meaning of what Jesus did on the cross.

Although the Bible does contain nonnarrative teaching, it starts with and majors on stories. The nonnarrative commentary and application of the stories mostly happens in the second half of the New Testament. What does this suggest in terms of where we should start teaching?

Old Testament Storytelling

There are a few examples of how teaching was conducted in the Old Testament. We know that in Ezra and Nehemiah's time, the Law was read out and various Levites commented on it (Neh 8:7). Interestingly, Nehemiah 9 describes a prayer led by a group of Levites—a prayer that relies on storying. The prayer tells the story of Abraham (Neh 9:7-8), the exodus and the Red Sea (Neh 9:9-12) and Sinai (Neh 9:13). Then it goes on to tell of the rebellions in the desert and how God still sustained his people (Neh 9:16-21), the conquest (Neh 9:22-25) and finally the exile (Neh 9:26-37).

We need to remember that the Israelites were brought up on the stories of God's dealings with them. For example, their main festival was Passover. This celebration included a retelling within the family context of how God saved them. The story was undergirded by the food they ate—roast lamb, unleavened bread and bitter herbs. All were reminders of their great salvation story. The roast lamb reminded them of the perfect lamb that was slain and whose blood on the doorposts signified that they'd obeyed God—thus their eldest son was saved. The symbolism of the unleavened bread wasn't explained at the time. It may have been partially a reminder of the need to be ready for a speedy deliverance since the yeast wouldn't have had time to work (Ex 12:11). We tend to think of the yeast as relating to sin, but this may be an unrelated idea from the New Testament (Mk 8:15; 1 Cor 5:6-8). The bitter herbs were probably a reminder of the bitterness of the slavery they were rescued from. Thus, when these events were referred to in prayers or other contexts, the whole story flooded into the listener's mind. This process is similar to what we experience when someone says, "She was an ugly duckling." If you don't know the story, you're probably puzzled. But if you do know it, you understand that a girl was unattractive when young and then one day, to everyone's surprise, she flowered into a great beauty.

The Pentateuch, or the first five books of the Old Testament, is often called "the book of the Law" and is attributed to Moses' authorship. While based on that description we might expect to find it a list of laws, in fact more than half is narrative. And even the laws recorded are all in the context of the grand salvation story. The book of Deuteronomy is Moses' farewell address to the people. Chapters 1–4 are the story of the spies and the people's refusal to enter the land. Chapters 9–10 contain the story of the golden calf and how the stone tablets had to be replaced. When Moses speaks his last words, in chapters 11–34, he chooses to combine styles using both storying and other teaching forms. Similarly, various psalms (Ps 78; 105; 106; 135; 136) follow the model of singing the stories of Israel's history. Through song the stories are reviewed and continue to deepen their impact on people's hearts.

There are other Old Testament storytellers, but I will close with Hosea. Hosea is unusual because his book of prophecy takes the form of an enacted story. Hosea is told, "Go, take to yourself an adulterous wife and children of unfaithfulness, because the land is guilty of the vilest adultery in departing from the Lord" (Hos 1:2). Later this wife, Gomer, runs away, and again God speaks to Hosea: "Go, show your love to your wife again, though she is loved by another and is an adulteress. Love her as the LORD loves the Israelites, though they turn to other gods" (Hos 3:1). This acted-out prophecy is tremendously powerful. I found even as a teenager that this prophet's message was easily remembered since the story provides the framework for the prophecy. And the main points of God's message to his people are embedded in the story itself.

Jesus the Storyteller

Jesus is the ultimate model of how to teach. Even a cursory reading of Matthew, Mark, Luke and John shows that Jesus' basic verbal teaching method was storytelling—so much so that the word "parable" has come to be associated strongly with Jesus. For him, not using a story was the exception.

Let's look at Jesus' teaching on prayer. Initially Jesus modeled prayer, but eventually the disciples asked him to teach them to pray. So he taught them a prayer in outline form and offered them teaching on certain points, such as, don't pray in public like the Pharisees do for the praise for others. However, nearly all the rest of his teaching on prayer is in the form of stories. For example, the story of the son asking his father for bread: What father would give his son a stone? Jesus sums up the stories by saying, "If you, then, though you are evil, know how to give good gifts to your children, how much more will your Father in heaven give good gifts to those who ask him!" (Mt 7:11). He also tells the parable of the persistent widow (Lk 18:1-8) "to show them that they should always pray and not give up" (Lk 18:1). Then he offers the parable of the Pharisee and tax collector (Lk 18:9-14) to show the kind of humble attitude God accepts.

What's interesting is that Jesus offers stories in situations where we might be tempted to jump to abstract teaching. For example, when Peter approaches Jesus and asks, "How many times shall I forgive my brother when he sins against me? Up to seven times?" (Mt 18:21), Jesus gives a one-sentence direct answer: "I tell you, not seven times, but seventy-seven times" (Mt 18:22). He then launches into the remaining ninety percent of his answer, which is the powerful story of the unmerciful servant. He concludes with, "This is how my heavenly Father will treat each of you unless you forgive your brother from your heart" (Mt 18:35).

Jesus also delivers many of his criticisms of the Pharisees through stories. The Pharisee and tax collector story is told for the benefit of those "confident of their own righteousness" (Lk 18:9). The story of the two men who owed debts, one huge and one miniscule, and who were both forgiven is told to Simon the Pharisee. In his heart Simon despised the sinful woman and thought himself better (Lk 7:36-50), but Jesus wanted him to realize that "he who has been forgiven little loves little" (Lk 7:47). Jesus tells stories of unfaithful tenants and people who rejected invitations to wedding banquets (Mt 21:33-46; 22:1-14) and stories of sheep and goats to warn that God judges the heart, not the outside, and he can't be fooled (Mt 25:31-46). The fact that the Pharisees understood Jesus' criticisms is evident by their angry responses (Mt 21:45-46). Delivering the rebukes in the form of stories ensured that Jesus' listeners stayed to hear the whole rebuke.

After the resurrection Jesus talks to two men on the road to Emmaus (Lk 24:13-35). These men are grieving and confused because their expectations about Jesus weren't met. They believed that God incarnate would never die; rather he'd be victorious and bring in the kingdom of God (like most, they thought of this process only in physical, earthly terms). They don't recognize Jesus, either because they're not expecting him or they're kept from recognizing him until they understand the Scriptures better. Jesus, beginning with "Moses and all the Prophets, . . . explained to them what was said in all the Scriptures concerning himself" (Lk 24:27). Did Jesus do this in a storying form? It is not clear. This is one of those times I wish more were recorded.

Peter, Stephen and Paul in Acts

The book of Acts contains several of the early church leaders' sermons. These sermons are probably only outlines; most likely they were significantly longer than what is recorded. Peter's sermon on the day of Pentecost (Acts 2) uses storying to link the prophecies of David and Joel to the story of Jesus. Peter had an advantage in that his audience was much more familiar with the Old Testament than modern people are, so he could dive right in and spend more time on the coming of the Messiah, which fulfills what his hearers knew of the Old Testament.

Peter's sermon at the Beautiful Gate (Acts 3:11-26) is a similar style. The bare outline progresses from the promises to Abraham and covers Moses, Samuel and other prophets, then comes to the story of Jesus and how he was handed over to be killed by the very people he came to save. If this sermon outline is recorded in the order it was spoken, we can see that sometimes it's a good idea to start the story at the end and work backward. That is, we can start exactly where a person is in life and fill in the background before moving forward. It depends on the situation. We might start at Noah or Abraham or Moses because someone's question naturally pushes us to start there, but we can ask permission to go earlier and fill in the rest so our listener understands more completely.

This is likely the pattern Philip followed when he explained the gospel to the Ethiopian eunuch in Acts 8. The conversation starts with the eunuch reading parts of Isaiah 53 and asking, "Who is the prophet talking about, himself or someone else?" We're told, "Then Philip began with that very passage . . . and told him the good news about Jesus" (Acts 8:34-35). It would have been foolish for Philip to say, "First I must tell you about Genesis 1." The eunuch would have had trouble listening. He would have wanted to say, "But that wasn't my question. I want to know what this Isaiah passage means!" My guess is that Philip first told the eunuch that the passage was about the Savior. Then it would have been logical for him to find out what the man knew about the coming Savior. This would have been the time to go back to the beginning of the story and, once he got back to Isaiah, move forward to Jesus.

Peter uses storying with Cornelius and his family. This family seems to have had some familiarity with biblical truth because they're described as "God-fearing" (Acts 10:2). But their knowledge is limited. We know this not only because God directly intervenes to help them come to know him fully, but they try to bow to Peter as though he were a god (Acts 10:25). Only ten verses of Peter's message to Cornelius are recorded, but he seems to have majored on the story of Jesus, including his miracles, death, resurrection, return and final commands. Peter also mentions that the prophets pointed to Jesus (Acts 10:43), and I suspect (though I can't prove) that Peter referred back to various of those prophecies, because this was the model he received from the resurrected Jesus (see Lk 24), and it seemed to be his pattern in Acts 2 and 3.

Paul is not someone with whom we naturally associate the word "storyteller." Yet the examples we have of his sermons—again, probably only outlines—contain storying. One longer sermon is recorded in a synagogue in Pisidian Antioch on his first missionary journey (Acts 13:13-41). Paul starts with the exodus (Acts 13:17), moves on to the conquest (13:19) and then covers Saul and David (13:20-22) before moving on to Jesus. Paul then returns to the prophecies of David and Isaiah to back up what he's said about Jesus.

In Thessalonica we have only hints that Paul used storying: "On three Sabbath days he reasoned with them from the Scriptures, explaining and proving that the Christ had to suffer and rise from the dead" (Acts 17:2-3). Based on his earlier sermons, it seems likely that Paul wove the stories and prophecies of the Old Testament into the story of Jesus. These Jews already knew the stories of Israel's history, which allowed Paul to briefly mention them and then move forward. In contrast, the Athens sermon in the Areopagus (Acts 17:22-34) is delivered to non-Jews. And so Paul changes his approach. First he connects with his listeners by noting their religious zeal. Then he starts storying, but he assumes no Old Testament background. He starts from creation and moves toward the resurrection.

Twice Paul uses his own testimony when he speaks (Acts 22; 26), weaving in what he has learned about Jesus and how he has come to understand the prophecies of the Old Testament. I wish we had more of Paul's sermon outlines. It seems to me that our modern preaching claims to take Paul as a model, but really it's taking his written letters as a model rather than what we know of his spoken teaching. Many sermons are abstract and are unmemorable. For example, contrast a sermon on the theme of "God loves you and wants you to come back to him" with "There was a father who had two sons. . . . The younger said to his father, 'Give me my share of the estate.' Not long after that the younger son got together all he had, set off for a distant land and there squandered his wealth in wild living. . . . While he was still a long way off, his father saw him . . . ran to him . . . threw his arms around him and kissed him" (Lk 15:11-32).

A few years ago I attended a weeklong conference that used the storying method to look at Elijah. Years later I can still remember all the stories in detail and the main points of teaching. How many sermon series can we say that about? I also recently heard two sermons over two days from an experienced British preacher. The first one featured an elegant outline on Ephesians. I wrote it down because I thought I could use it. The next day he preached on Genesis 15 in story form. I remembered nothing from the first sermon even a day later. Months later I can still tell you what the storying sermon was about, and it is still influencing my life. What would happen if we went back to storytelling through books of the Bible, commenting on and applying the stories to our lives? What would happen if we used the teaching in letters as backup to the stories rather than the reverse? Would our listeners remember God's Word better?

The clearest example of storying in Acts is in Stephen's sermon to the Sanhedrin in Acts 7. Stephen starts with a relatively detailed rendition of Abraham's story. This story is the logical starting point for Jews because they already knew and accepted the creation story. They didn't need to rehear it as did the pagan Athenians, who didn't believe that one God created the world. Stephen then creates a bridge through the Jacob-Joseph story into the Moses story. He goes into lots of detail (Acts 7:20-44), then proceeds to Joshua and the tabernacle. We must remember that

Stephen's audience is familiar with these stories. Yet they are gripped by what Stephen says and allow him to speak for a long time. Stephen's point is that throughout the Jews' history, they've rejected and resisted God. He makes his point so successfully that his audience stones him to shut him up! The fact that Stephen is able to speak so long is probably linked with his storying style. It carries people along and sneaks under their defenses until the finale drives the point home and makes them so furious that they gnash their teeth in fury (Acts 7:54).

Where do we choose to start our teaching? How often do we choose to speak from the narrative sections of the Bible? Even a brief survey of Old and New Testament teaching and evangelism models shows that storytelling was a major method in Scripture. The more I've used narrative, the more people have remembered what I've taught. As a coworker of mine said in a seminar, "If God chose to pack his divine book full of stories, and trusted the power of those stories to change people's worldview, then why do we insist on reducing the gospel and Christian teaching to sets of propositional truth statements?"[1]

Reflection

1. What are the sermons and Bible lessons that you still remember after many years?

2. What points in this chapter challenge you?

3. What stories in the Bible most clearly explain our sin?

4. What stories most clearly explain other aspects of the gospel, such as forgiveness? Grace? Substitution?

PART TWO

PREPARING A BASIC
STORY SET

CHOOSING SUITABLE STORIES

Remember Amanda, the Taiwanese girl who went to church with a friend and struggled with the speaker's abstract teaching style? Well, she eventually came to Christ through hearing a set of fourteen stories and reading the Bible afterward to fill in the gaps and add more details. As part of her discipleship process I wanted Amanda to start learning the stories and using them with her friends. When I told her this, she went into a minor panic. The stories had taken several months to tell. How could she possibly learn so many? This is a common reaction. People feel overwhelmed by the size of the task. For many of us, this is enough to prevent us from even making a start.

This chapter aims to break the task down into small steps and give you the tools to start working on a basic set of stories you can use in evangelism. I was tempted to place my own basic set in this book, but I resisted, both because I didn't want "my" stories to become a lesser Bible and because it will help you more to prepare a set yourself. This process should also help make the stories suitable for your cultural context.

One reason I struggled with including a basic story set in this book is that I started with someone else's basic set. But I had to make fairly major adjustments to the original stories I received before I started using them effectively. Sanchez, Terry and Thompson warn against generic story sets. They make clear that the "failures" people experience with storying are most often due to the fact that they use generic stories that aren't suited to the worldview of the listener. That is, their failure is not because "storying doesn't work" but because of how they've applied the method.[1] The extra effort you expend to develop a tailor-made set for your own situation will also greatly assist you when you start training others.

No matter what your cultural context there are basic principles in the process of selecting stories to tell. Here they are.

Step 1: Map Out Your Hearers' Worldview

The more familiar we are with our listeners' beliefs, the better we are equipped to select stories that challenge those beliefs. The stories we choose and the way we share them should be different for every listener. Even within one culture or religious background we must not assume that everyone's beliefs are uniform. Especially in today's world, there is a complex mixing of beliefs even within religions that used to have clearly delineated doctrines. A concrete way to think about worldview is this "brick wall" illustration:

It is as if every person is surrounded by a brick wall. The bricks are thick and prevent us from hearing what someone is saying outside the wall. Each brick represents something we believe is true about life. Often our wall is built mostly of lies and we don't even know it. For example, many Westerners have a "brick" that says that science and belief in God are mutually exclusive. They may also believe that the Bible is unreliable and contains many contradictions. Asians may believe that Christianity is a Western religion and therefore has no relevance to them. They may also be convinced that all religions are equally valid without considering the inherent contradictions of their belief.

Both nonbelievers and believers have many false bricks. God will take a lifetime challenging them. Our goal in storying is to choose stories that target the bricks in a person's life. Of course, we ourselves can't change a single brick. Only God has the power to do that. But our hope is that a person's wall of lies will become a wall of truth. This wall then is no longer a barrier but a protection. As Satan shoots his lies at us (Eph 6:16), we'll be able to differentiate truth from lies and be protected.

This image doesn't define the number of bricks that need to change before someone becomes a Christian. The line between evangelism and discipleship is often blurred. Some people believe quickly and then are discipled. Others will think through many issues that we might consider subjects for Christians before they decide to follow Jesus for themselves. That is, much discipleship happens before they trust Jesus. Although we may possess a basic set of evangelistic stories, we will always adjust them to suit the "bricks" of the individual. Sometimes the Holy Spirit will guide us to tell a totally different story than what we were originally planning.

Action step 1. Prepare a brick wall diagram for your cultural context or the context of the person you're storying with. Even if the person is a Westerner, you will find that he or she has a unique cultural background. This person might be an Irish or Italian Roman Catholic or a Lutheran from northern Europe. Or this person might be a completely secular atheist or agnostic. Make the brick wall diagram as detailed as possible. You might find that you need to ask questions to discover views on life after death, the origins of human life, how to be saved, the supernatural world, and the existence of God or gods. Also consider the worship systems the person comes from:

- Why does he worship? What kind of requests does he make when he prays?
- Does she worship at a special place and with special rituals?
- Who can join the worship? Who leads it?
- Is worship individual or communal? Is it done in families?
- Does he worship out of joy, desperation, fear or something else?

For example, in Taiwan some worship takes place at temples, but it is essentially an individual experience involving set rituals. Sometimes families go together. Taiwanese people generally go to a temple only on a special day, such as a god's birthday, or if they want something such as health, wealth, good relationships or success in exams. Thanksgiving, praise and any kind of family relationship with the god are rare. Several roadside sellers in Taiwan with whom I've been sharing stories recently told me, "Our prayer is all about manipulation to get what we want. When you pray to your God, you praise him and ask him what he wants you to do!"

Action step 2. Try to identify which "bricks" are the major barriers in your cultural context. For example, in some Western contexts people might believe that faith is blind, thus Christianity is for fools. Or they might believe that religion is unscientific. This will prevent them from even starting to investigate.

In Taiwan, three major barriers come up during evangelism, two early and one later. Usually within the first gospel conversations people say, "All religions are the same." This can be a genuine belief that all religions are alike because they encourage people to be "good." It may also be a way of avoiding further conversation, or of saying, "I'm not interested and don't want to think." They sometimes make this explicit by expressing a second barrier:

"Christianity is a Western religion." This most often happens if they're speaking with a Westerner, which is a strong reason for having locals do the storying. Later, the issue of ancestor worship comes up. Christians are viewed as unfilial, almost haters of their families, because they won't do the approved practices of offering incense and food to deceased ancestors.

Ingrid told her grandfather the creation story. He immediately voiced one of his "bricks": "Christianity is a Western religion. I don't want to hear about it." Ingrid asked, "Did God only create Westerners?" After a little more discussion, her grandfather admitted that if God really was the creator, then following him was for everybody. Tackling this misunderstanding so early meant that her grandfather was willing to listen further. Major bricks will have to be tackled again and again through the process of storying and discussion.

Action step 3. Identify any gospel "bridges" within the culture or situation. In Acts 8 Philip is instructed by an angel, "Go south to the road—the desert road—that goes down from Jerusalem to Gaza" (Acts 8:26). When he arrives he sees an Ethiopian eunuch who turns out to be an important official in charge of the queen's treasury. The Holy Spirit tells Philip, "Go to that chariot and stay near it" (Acts 8:29). As Philip obeys he hears the man reading part of Isaiah 53. Philip asks, "Do you understand what you're reading?"

"How can I, unless someone explains it to me?" he replies (Acts 8:30-31). So Philip gets into the chariot and explains the gospel to the eunuch starting from that passage.

This Ethiopian somehow already knows enough about God to respect him and come on a lengthy journey to worship him. It's likely that he has a basic biblical background, so Philip doesn't immediately start from creation with him but from the point where he is unclear. The result is that the man immediately grasps the pieces of the puzzle he's been missing and asks to be baptized.

Some cultures have traditions or stories that prepare the way for the gospel. Russell and Barbara Reed, American missionaries with OMF International, wanted to be part of God's eternal plan. So in 1953 they went to the Philippines. After learning the national language, they set out to reach the Batangan, a tribal group on the island of Mindoro. For six months the Reeds searched for the people on the east side of Mindoro. Eventually they found a Batangan village and started learning the language. Several years later the people showed initial interest in the gospel, but after several deaths occurred, that interest was replaced with fear and rejection. Then a related language group seemed to show tentative interest, but again it amounted to nothing.

After nine years in the Philippines, the Reeds had not seen one tribal person make a commitment, although they'd started Bible translation. That changed in May 1962. Traveling to the east again, they found a group of people with hungry hearts. Before long, seventy-five people were baptized, almost the entire adult population of three villages. What made the difference? Centuries earlier a shaman had prophesied, "Someday, white people will come here to teach us. Big people. And they will know our language. When they come, we must follow their teaching." This prophecy was passed down for sixteen generations. When the leader in the east heard the Reeds speaking his language, he knew they were the ones for whom his tribe had waited more than three hundred and fifty years.[2]

Consider also whether there are traditional stories or proverbs that can be bridges. The Taiwanese have a proverb about a frog in the bottom of a well. When he looks up he can see only one patch of sky and concludes that it's the whole sky. People are like that. Our view is limited. It is when we come to know the creator of the universe that he allows us to see more of the sky and understand the world better. This proverb can be used to start a whole series of stories because we are claiming that the stories allow us to see how huge the sky really is.

Here's a saying from the Democratic Republic of Congo: "During a storm you do not take shelter under just one roofing tile." This could be a good lead-in to talk about whether the things we rely on are really useful in the storms of life. If our problems are bigger than what we depend on, why do we keep depending on it? We need to find something or someone greater than all our storms.

Also in an African context, the saying "a stubborn chicken learns its lesson in a hot pot of soup" would be a great start to telling the story of Nebuchadnezzar in Daniel 4. Stubborn people often have to suffer before they'll listen. Nebuchadnezzar had to go mad and eat grass like the cattle before he would "acknowledge that the Most High is sovereign over the kingdoms of men and gives them to anyone he wishes" (Dan 4:32). It's a good warning too to listen to God sooner rather than later and not have to face the "cooking pot."[3] The better we understand the worldview of those we're sharing with, the better we can communicate the gospel to them.

Step 2: Choose Stories That Challenge Beliefs
At this stage, list any stories you can think of that address the particular issues facing your hearers' worldview. You will not necessarily use all of these stories in your basic set. J. O. Terry suggests that sometimes deep-rooted beliefs need to be addressed by five to seven stories on the topic.[4] But these don't all have to be included in your basic set. Stories aren't a magic method. You won't tell one story and then suddenly see a person's whole worldview change. Stories are used by God in his timing and in his own ways.

Step 3: Choose Stories That Reveal God's Glory
The theme of God revealing his glory is one we can easily miss and fail to include in our stories. We can make our focus too small and consider salvation only in terms of personal salvation. God's view is substantially broader than that, and we need to reflect that. Why did God save Noah or choose Abraham? Why did he do the mighty wonders of the exodus and allow Pharaoh's heart to be hardened? It wasn't just to save individuals. There was a wider purpose. Sometimes this point is made explicitly in a

story. For example, in Exodus God tells Pharaoh through Moses, "By now I could have stretched out my hand and struck you and your people with a plague that would have wiped you off the earth. But I have raised you up for this very purpose, that I might show you my power and that my name might be proclaimed in all the earth" (Ex 9:15-16).

So in choosing stories, first think through the whole sweep of the Bible and write down any stories you think are suitable. It doesn't matter whether the list is long. Once you have a long list, think about how each story relates to your listeners' worldview. Check that you have enough stories so that there are not strange gaps. Also think about the fact that some stories are foundational to help people more fully understand Jesus' identity and his role. For example, stories about the tabernacle and the Day of Atonement set up the crucifixion story.

A group of new missionaries were making lists of possible stories. Aside from the expected selections, they included such stories as Jonah and Ruth. The question was whether these stories were necessary in the basic set or could be used in follow-up. Were they essential in understanding Jesus and his salvation purpose? Different personalities and cultural contexts will influence the kinds of stories we choose. We will gravitate to stories that have moved us personally or challenged our own spiritual walk. Look at your list and ask which stories are essential for an evangelistic set.

Step 4: Not Too Long, Not Too Short, but Just Right

Think through your cultural context in terms of how long people will listen to a story set. It is no use having a "basic set" of fifty stories if no one has the patience or time to sit through them all. The chronological Bible storying approach was developed in tribal contexts where people didn't have electricity or television. The listeners were delighted to gather every night and listen for an hour. Most storytellers would love such a situation. But in modern contexts it is far more common for people to be overly busy. Many people no longer have breathing space to ask deep questions and to think. Therefore a story set has to fit into realistic expectations. My first set was divided into seven sections. Now I have a fourteen-section set (I'm in less of a rush nowadays), but the five to six stories of Jesus' ministry can be done in one session if needed because each story is short.

A basic set usually contains about twelve to twenty stories—it depends on how you calculate them. I call my Abraham story one story, but in fact it is about five separate stories. If one of the stories on the list distracts from the primary salvation story, consider using it as the start of another set or just as a separate follow-up story. Don't be afraid to have half to two-thirds of your stories be from the Old Testament. The Old Testament stories set up the New Testament and prepare the way for the Savior.

All basic story sets will have some stories in common. However, the exact way we tell these basic stories will depend on our cultural context. Storytellers will also develop their own methods for starting a story series. They'll have "signature" stories that become their favorite ways to get started. A basic set would almost certainly contain the following:

Old Testament:

1. Creation (Genesis 1–2)
2. Rebellion (Genesis 3)
3. Abraham (Genesis 12–24)
4. The exodus and Passover (Exodus 1–12)

New Testament:

1. Jesus' birth as a fulfillment of prophecy
2. Jesus' ministry
3. Crucifixion
4. Resurrection

Old Testament Stories

Besides the stories of creation, the fall and the life of Abraham, here are some Old Testament Bible stories that could be included in a basic set:

Noah. I include the story of the flood in my basic set for two main reasons. First, it's a story that many people have heard or that exists in some form in their culture. For example, the Mongolians have a story of a huge flood. Second, it is a "two choices, two results" story. If you listen to God and choose to trust him (even when you don't fully understand), you'll be saved. If you refuse to listen, the result is judgment and destruction. This helps people realize that there are only two ways to respond to God. There is no middle way.

Sinai. The final Old Testament section is where the most personal choice comes into play, and it is the section you'll probably struggle with most. You might include the Red Sea story because, again, it is well-known and it illustrates how quickly the Israelites forgot that God could save them. Another way to divide these stories is to tell the first nine plagues one week, then the following week tell the tenth plague, Passover and Red Sea story. It varies depending on the needs of the listener and his or her available time. I do quite a bit of storytelling in the market. Customers interrupt frequently, so flexibility is necessary to determine how long each story section should be. Often they need to be shorter.

I have at times combined this story with a change of pace by watching a movie like DreamWorks' *The Prince of Egypt* for one session. Using different media can be beneficial. After the movie, sometimes I start a discussion about why the moviemakers altered bits of the story. For example, the theme song eulogizes the power of belief but suggests that the belief is in oneself, while the biblical story is about the power of trusting in an almighty God—a fundamental difference. If you use this approach, you might first tell your listeners the story, then have them read the entire biblical account on their own before watching the movie.

That way they become familiar with the true standard, God's Word, before watching the movie, which is an interpretation of the original story.

I've been surprised at the number of people even in Taiwan who have seen the old movie *The Ten Commandments*, starring Charlton Heston. When we reach the Sinai stories, they immediately recognize it and another piece of the puzzle falls into place. They may also suddenly realize that this is history and not just a movie. Sometimes a musical, play, work of art, song or movie can help solidify a biblical story in someone's mind. Plus, a different storying format engages different kinds of learners. However, if a particular art form turns out to be a distraction in your context, then you quickly learn not to use it again.

A word of warning: Although it's a popular story, the Ten Commandments account can be misinterpreted and result in people trying to rely on works. It's only when the commandments are told in context (Exodus 20:2 gives an-all important context hint) that we realize the commandments are principles for the people of God (those already saved), showing how far we are from God's standards and how desperately we need a Savior. So a story like the Ten Commandments might work better as part of a later discipleship set or as a way to demonstrate how high God's standards are.

Currently my Sinai story includes the Israelites' coming to the mountain and God's revealing of himself on the mountaintop. I simply say that the Israelites responded in fear and begged Moses to represent them and talk to God (Ex 19:16-19; 20:18-19). Then I talk about how God wanted the people to worship him. I highlight God's holiness and perfect standards. The tabernacle and Day of Atonement sections prepare the way for Jesus' birth and death. Finally, I tell the golden calf story (Ex 32) because it suits the Taiwanese situation. This story tackles the issue of idolatry but in an indirect way. The Israelites seem to have thought they weren't worshiping other gods but were using a representation of God so they could worship him better (Ex 32:4). The problem was that no image can ever represent God because any object insults and limits him. There is no object in the created world that is great enough.

Some storytellers finish their Old Testament stories with a reference to the prophets, particularly the prophecies about the coming Savior. I mention the prophets in their role of calling people to repentance as the end of my Old Testament set. I start the New Testament set with a mention of two main prophecies about the Savior—his mother would be a virgin and he would be born in Bethlehem—and state that there was a gap of four hundred to seven hundred years of waiting. Then I tell the story about Jesus' birth, starting with "One day an angel appeared to a young virgin called Mary. . . ."

Jesus' Ministry Stories

Once you've reached the New Testament, stories about Jesus' ministry are one way you can really tackle worldview issues. I use five stories about Jesus' authority.[5] I introduce the stories by saying that Jesus chose twelve disciples (or students) to live and work with him. Then I use one story each to demonstrate Jesus' authority over sickness, demons, nature, death and sin. This gives a good overview of his miracles. The miracle stories concurrently emphasize Jesus' authority as a teacher.

Stories can achieve multiple purposes within one account. The first story in the authority of Jesus series I tell is from Luke 13:10-17, which tells of the healing of a woman crippled by an evil spirit. The Gospels contain many healing stories. Why choose this one? It introduces the topic of evil spirits. That means I'll have an opportunity to talk about evil spirits and Satan—important in any culture but particularly non-Western cultures. I'll also have to admit that I don't fully understand the link between the spirit and the woman's crippling. It is good for us to demonstrate that we don't have to have all the answers to trust Christ. (There's also a possibility that our hearers will understand these things better than us, which will enable them to be the "teacher" and us the learner—the roles aren't always as obvious as we think.) The story of the woman with the evil spirit also offers glimpses of the issues in the religious leaders' hearts and why they later wanted to kill Jesus. In addition, it shows Jesus looking out for the weak and rejected.

Mark 1:21-28 highlights not only Jesus' authority over demons but also his authority as a teacher and the fact that the demons recognize who Jesus is when the people and religious leaders don't. Jesus' calming of the storm is probably the clearest example of his authority over nature. It certainly scared the disciples and made them ask, "Who is this? Even the wind and waves obey him" (Mk 4:41). I used to tell the story of the raising of Jairus's daughter because it was easy, but I've recently used the Lazarus story from John 11. Although the raising of Lazarus is a complex story, it highlights why the Pharisees wanted to kill Jesus—he was becoming too popular and influential—and the beginning of the plot to do so.

Another story I love to tell fourth or fifth in this set of five is from Mark 2:1-12. Jesus is teaching in Capernaum, his home area. Crowds arrive and totally surround him so that there is no room left. Four men carry their paralyzed friend on his mat toward Jesus but they can't even get close to him. So they go onto the roof, dig through it and then lower their friend down right in front of Jesus. Jesus says, "Son, your sins are forgiven."

> Some teachers of the law were sitting there, thinking to themselves, "Why does this fellow talk like that? He's blaspheming! Who can forgive sins but God alone?"
>
> Immediately Jesus knew in his spirit that this was what they were thinking in their hearts, and he said to them, "Why are you thinking these things? Which is easier: to say to the paralytic, 'Your sins are forgiven,' or to say, 'Get up, take your mat and walk'? But that you may know that the Son of Man has authority on earth to forgive sins . . . " He

said to the paralytic, "I tell you, get up, take your mat and go home." He got up, took his mat and walked out in full view of them all. This amazed everyone and they praised God, saying, "We have never seen anything like this!" (Mk 2:6-12)

You might choose all your New Testament stories from the Gospel of Luke so that you can follow up by watching the *Jesus* film. You may decide to share several parables. These stories aren't easy to interpret, and so people will often need to hear several before they learn to see the spiritual meanings behind them. In an initial salvation history set for evangelism purposes, it's best to choose parables that underline God's character and the need for salvation. Many people love the story of the good Samaritan, but it is easily misunderstood, even by the storyteller. It can degenerate into a story that tells us to be "good." The whole message of the Bible is that we can't be good! We can never reach God's perfect standards.

Jesus' teaching in the Sermon on the Mount is meant to help his listeners realize this point. Many in the crowd were self-satisfied, thinking they'd kept the commandments, but Jesus showed them that it's more about attitude—hating someone and being angry is the equivalent of murdering that person (Mt 5:21-22). He wanted his hearers to reach the point of saying, "But we can't keep them! Help!" This leads naturally into stories of the crucifixion and resurrection, underscoring the importance of why Jesus' sacrifice was necessary.

The Resurrection Story

This story could run from Luke 24:1 through Acts 1:11 when we consider that Luke wrote his Gospel and the book of Acts as a two-volume set. This allows us to include the return of Jesus to heaven and the final task he gave his followers on earth. Plus, it includes the notion that Jesus will return. The giving of the Holy Spirit can also be mentioned as God coming to be with us. This leads naturally into a set on Acts. This second set works well with believers or those who have heard many other stories and need to be challenged to embrace the cost and joy of following Jesus.

I have been telling stories to some street sellers in Taiwan who are afraid to follow Jesus—afraid of rejection by their families and afraid of being called unfilial. After several sets of stories, I started Acts. Although these men can see that following Jesus is difficult, they've also noted that the believers were willing to die for their beliefs because knowing Jesus is more important even than life. I'm hoping this will reduce their fears to a proper size. They've also noticed that even in death, the Holy Spirit was present with Jesus' followers and helped them face death with courage.

In the end it doesn't really matter exactly which stories you choose because all of God's Word is powerful. But it is worth thinking through which ones will work best in your situation. Be prepared to change your mind. And don't forget to pray; we need the Holy Spirit to guide us toward the best stories. Once you've worked out the stories in your set, how do you actually go about preparing them to share? We'll look at that question next.

Reflection

1. If you haven't already, create a brick wall diagram for your cultural context and worldview. Then create two lists: a long list of possible stories to tackle the "bricks" and a shorter list of stories to include in your basic salvation set.

2. Ask yourself if each story needs to be included the basic salvation set or if it should be in a later set. Once you have your basic set, ask yourself whether there is a logical flow to the stories.

3. Pray, pray, pray. This is hard but important work.

4

PREPARING STORIES FROM THE BIBLICAL TEXT

I recently worked with a group of people who were learning about storying and preparing their first story from the biblical text. At first the preparation process seemed somewhat slow and artificial. But the next session they prepared another story and the process was faster. Within a few days, the group could prepare complicated stories without referring to their notes. Once the basic set of stories is part of your life, learning other sets will become easier.

In this chapter we'll start with thinking about how to prepare a short story and then move on to how to prepare a story set and even turn a whole book of the Bible into a set of stories. (Note: I haven't included transcripts of actual stories in this book since they should really be experienced orally rather than in print. But you can listen to examples of storying online at storyingthescriptures.com.)

Preparing a Single Story: Basic Steps

Pray first. Praying reminds us that each story is part of God's Word and that it's important to be accurate and careful with it. We can pray not only for the preparation process but also for the people who will hear this portion of the Bible.

Read the Bible story. Most people find they need to read a story at least three times. Read it out loud at least once—this slows you down and helps you notice and focus on the details and dialogue. If the story is long and you're concerned about being able to remember it, draw a cartoon strip. Four to eight pictures are usually enough. You'll probably need to look at the cartoons only a few times before you can do without them. The cartoons are designed as a memory prompt for yourself. Don't take them with you when you start telling the stories—they'll distract both you and your listeners. Just keep practicing until you are confident without them.

A sample cartoon strip. Below is a cartoon strip I developed for the creation story. This cartoon is deliberately drawn with day four under day one, day five under day two, and day six under day three. This is because each picture relates to the one above or below it. First there are three separations: light and dark, sky and sea, sea and dry land. Then the creation starts. Day four fills the heavens with bodies of light. Day five fills the skies and sea, and day six fills the dry land with animals and humans. The only day that breaks this pattern is day three, when plants are created immediately when there is dry ground for them to grow on.

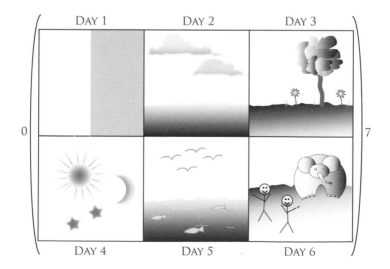

The brackets are my way of saying that the story has a beginning and an end. The beginning is the line noted as "0," for which I say something like, "The universe was originally formless and dark. Only God's Spirit was present, hovering over the waters." Day seven is the conclusion, and I simply say, "On day seven, God rested because he had completed the work of creation."

Tell the story out loud. If you don't practice out loud, you'll tend to mentally skip the hard bits and then won't be confident enough to tell others the story. Many people who learn storying have a great desire to read or hear the story and take notes to help them remember what to say. I've found that this is not the best way to remember. Practicing out loud is the best way.

Close your Bible. You'll probably feel an overwhelming desire to check the details of the story. Resist it at this stage. If you return to the text too often early on, you'll tend to add too many details. This makes it hard for people to listen and discourages them from thinking they can tell stories themselves. I know closing the Bible is extremely difficult. I constantly find trainees sneaking looks at the Bible or keeping it open on their laps and reading parts of it. This inhibits the storytelling process. In addition, the more you work from written texts, the more you tend to memorize the story, and that's not the goal.

What? The Stories Aren't Memorized?

Yes, that's right. The stories are *not* memorized. Every time you tell the story it should be slightly different depending on your audience. You'll adapt the detail, the level of language and kind of language used, and your tone. For example, telling stories to elderly ladies will be different from telling stories to teenagers or young children. Men are different as well. These adaptations are what make storytelling an art and not a science. The ability to adapt will come with practice.

One common misunderstanding is that memorization is better. In fact, memorization means that we are not only limited by our memory but that we fail to impact our listeners. Memorizing means we become a "talking book." A memorized story will have all the limitations of the printed word. That is:

- It will sound like it is the final word on how things are done.

- It will communicate only to the one audience it was memorized for.

- We'll be limited by whether we're tired or nervous—it will be easy to forget and we'll need constant practice to keep the memorized script in our head.

- It will become stale and boring firstly to us and then our listeners.

One storytelling trainer says, "We battle memorizing the words of Bible stories. Some people are good at memorizing, but it limits how many stories they will learn, how long they remember the story, and how much it encourages others to learn. Looking at a written version of the story moves people toward memorizing."[1] As Walter Ong emphasizes, professional storytellers don't memorize. Rather they use the "same formulas and themes . . . stitched together . . . differently in each rendition, even by the same [person], depending on the audience reaction, the mood of the [storyteller] or of the occasion."[2]

Actors often do something similar. They first memorize the script, but as they become more familiar with the characters, they can sense when the words aren't quite right. They'll adjust them to the character they're portraying and also sometimes to the listeners. Beginning actors and storytellers often sound like beginners because they stick so rigidly to the script. Experienced storytellers are more flexible and able to contextualize, and thus they communicate better.

Imagine yourself in the story. What we must learn to do is to visualize the story—to walk around within it as though we're present in it. In effect, when we tell a story we become the soundtrack for the mental video we see so that others can see it too. So close your eyes and spend at least five minutes walking around in your story. This seems to work best if you choose one of the characters and imagine things from his or her point of view. Ask yourself, "What did he see? What did she hear or smell? How did he feel when X, Y or Z happened?"

The first time I trained people to do this, it felt uncomfortable and I wondered how the trainees would respond. The group dubiously gave it a try. Afterward all of them, even the men, said, "That was worth doing. Don't cut that element from the training." Even if the imagining process doesn't change the content of your story it often influences something of its "flavor" or atmosphere. It will certainly influence what you discuss.

Check the details. The next step is to open your Bible and read through the story again, checking the exact details and deciding which ones are important. We can be afraid of details, fearing that they'll make the story difficult to listen to. But we don't want to dumb down a story. And within the story form, details are remembered more easily. Plus, they often underline that a story is history. For example, after the resurrection the disciples went fishing all night but didn't catch anything. Someone called to them from the shore, "Throw your net on the right side of the boat and you will find some" (Jn 21:6). Later the author noted that the net "was full of large fish, 153, but even with so many the net was not torn" (Jn 21:11). The details underline that this story is an eyewitness account. It is often these subtle details that convince people they're listening to history and not myth.

If the story has natural repetition in it, don't cut it out. I used to assume that repetition was boring, but now I see it more positively. For example, the creation story features something like a chorus. At the end of each day of creation, the text says, "God saw that it was good. And there was evening and there was morning on the Xth day." This reflects the original text, which is beautifully rhythmic and repetitive. Probably this was an oral story that was later written down. It enhances the storytelling process to keep those oral aspects. You can also use repetition in the story of Israel's exodus from Egypt to emphasize Pharaoh's stubbornness and pride: "But Pharaoh kept on saying, 'No!'" It may be worthwhile to experiment with telling a story in several ways and see which the listeners respond to best.

Finally, *tell the story to someone.* Nothing will help you more than getting out and practicing. Evaluate and work on any parts of the story that need improving. It will usually be obvious which sections need improving, but if you don't know, ask your listeners.

Learning from a Story Rather Than the Bible

There are certain situations, especially in oral cultures, where people don't learn stories from the Bible but rather from someone else. This can be dangerous. Someone in the group needs to be able to read and monitor that the stories remain true to the biblical text. There are three different methods for accomplishing this. You can use all three methods one after another or just one or two methods. Your choice will be influenced by how fast your listeners learn and the time you have available.

Method 1: Q&A. Immediately after a story is told, the facilitator asks a series of communal comprehension questions, such as, "Where does this story take place? Who is the story about? What does person A say to person B? What happens next?" And so on. This method is particularly useful with groups that lack confidence.

Method 2: Telling in groups. After a story is told, the rest of the group practices telling it to one another in smaller groups of four to six people. One person starts and then passes to the next person whenever he or she wants. This practice run helps you to remember bits you might otherwise forget because more minds are better than one. If a story is particularly difficult or the group wants to practice again, they retell the story together with everyone telling a different part each subsequent time. One advantage of this method is that it allows group members to gently correct others. This happens naturally as they say, "That wasn't quite right. It was Jesus who said to the man . . . "

Method 3: Telling in pairs. Each person tells the whole story through from beginning to end to another person, who then tells it back to the first person. Generally one of the pair is more confident and can go first, allowing the other person to hear the whole story again before it's his or her turn.

If all these three methods are combined, everyone will have heard the story multiple times from multiple tellers. The more repetition the better in terms of gaining confidence and remembering a story accurately.

Action step. Prepare the creation story using the methods suggested above. Once you feel reasonably happy with your story, start telling it. It's best to start telling your stories to someone soon after you prepare them. Literate people tend to want to prepare a whole set before they begin sharing. The problem is that most people can't remember so many at a time. Rather than reverting to writing down the stories, prepare one and use it until it flows spontaneously before you go on to prepare the next.

Deleting Details from Stories

Here are a few guidelines for deciding which details to leave out when you're preparing a story.

1. Keep names to a minimum. In my cultural context, names are a problem. Taiwanese people struggle with the names in the Bible because translators have chosen to use sound equivalents for biblical characters' names. This was probably the right decision, but the problem is that the names don't sound Chinese, so locals struggle to remember strings of syllables that are unlike any of their local names. I frequently just name the major characters: Adam, Eve (sometimes I just call them "the first man and woman"), Noah, Abraham (I don't mention Sarah's name or their name changes) and Moses. If the names are familiar in your context then feel free to use more of them.

2. Keep numbers to a minimum. In Noah's story, is it necessary to know how long the ark took to build or how long it rained or how long the people were in the ark? If we decide these details aren't important, we can talk about how the water kept rising and rising until it covered the highest mountains, then how it stopped raining and the water receded. One exception would be if you were talking to a group of boat enthusiasts. The dimensions of the ark would help them relate to the story.

3. Be careful with religious jargon. There are several ways to deal with the inevitable special religious terms that come up. One method is to let people know ahead of time what terms will be in your story. You can define them up front—for example, explain what a "synagogue" is. Another approach is to help people notice a specific word and start them thinking. If the story talks about Noah the "righteous man," you could ask, "What do you think this might mean?" Let your hearers make suggestions but don't tell them the answer. Let them know that the story will contain clues. Then come back to this discussion after the story.

Another method is to use simplified terms. For example, rather than using the term "tabernacle," I often talk about a "beautiful tent" that was set up so God's people could worship him in one place and not wherever they felt like it. This tent later became a permanent temple. I explain about the special room at the back that represented God's presence and the curtain that separated it off to represent the separation between a perfect holy God and a sinful people. Only once a year could one representative (a "middleman") go through the curtain. However, he had to specially prepare by washing and wearing pure white clothes and then take the blood of a perfect goat in. God would then forgive their sin.

Words like "Sabbath" could become "weekly day of rest." "Pharisees" could be "religious leaders." "Disciples" could be "students" or "followers." If you're going to use a term repeatedly, such as "repentance," explain it well and keep using it with its explanation. When you use the word "repentance," check each time that they remember it. You might act it out by walking in one direction ("my way") and then turning 180 degrees and walking "God's way."

Adding Details to Stories

This is something we need to think through carefully. I add to the creation story in order to expand the rather bland phrase "each according to their kinds." I talk about the different kinds of plants, birds, fish and animals. However, I don't list particular species but rather give descriptions and categories. This tends to stimulate people's imaginations and help them to really "see" the stories and find them interesting and relevant. Here is an example using plants and birds: "Some plants are so huge you almost can't see the top of them, but others are so small you need a microscope to see them. For some vegetables we eat the leaves, and for others we eat the stalks or roots. Some birds may look plain but sing beautifully, and others that look fantastic have harsh voices." I make a squawk at this point and add a little humor to the story.

If you're going to add to the story, you need to have a clear reason why you're doing it. It needs to enhance learning of truth, not dominate and overshadow the truth. If you add too much it detracts from the biblical story and may add error or nonbiblical emphases. Sadly, some people may even add to a story to enhance their own storytelling reputation. If you're not sure about adding a detail, check with reliable people who love God's Word. Commentaries and Bible dictionaries can also be helpful tools.

Starting Well

A single story or the first story in a series. One possibility for starting effectively is an abrupt start with no bridging at all. This is the probably the best way to start the creation story because it matches exactly the abruptness of the Bible's start. "In the beginning the universe was formless and dark, and God said, "Let there be light!" (see Gen 1:1-3). Another option is using a question to alert listeners that the story will be relevant. For example, "Where did such a complex and beautiful world come from?" A series on Jonah could begin, "What would you do if God asked you to go and warn of coming judgment on your worst enemies?" Or for Daniel, "How would you respond if God allowed your country to be overrun, and you were dragged into captivity and forced to learn a new language and have a name change?"

Subsequent stories in a series. The storyteller might summarize the previous story or, even better, you might ask listeners what they remember and whether someone can tell the previous story. This allows the storyteller to discover how much the listeners remember. Does the previous story need to be repeated? Often as you do this hearers will say, "Oh, I do remember," and they'll start interrupting with the remembered sections. Let them tell it. The group will usually naturally correct any mistakes and it becomes a group storytelling.

With story sets that follow through a book or section of the Bible, it works well to bridge into the story with a question that will prompt the listener to concentrate on finding the answer. For example, "Will God give up on King Nebuchadnezzar? Will Nebuchadnezzar learn to trust God personally?" (prior to the Daniel 3 or 4 story). In actually starting the story it is usually just a matter of saying, "Soon after" or "Decades passed," and then launching into the story.

However, what about story sets like a basic Bible overview where there might be decades or centuries between the story sections? There must be some hint of this chronology. One simple way is to use a stock phrase like "Generations passed" or "Noah had sons and their sons had sons and so on for many generations." At the beginning of the exodus story, which comes after the Abraham story in my set, I usually say, "Abraham had

Isaac. In the time of Isaac's grandsons there was a famine in the land. The whole family moved to Egypt and there they multiplied for four hundred years." This bridges easily into the start of the biblical account in Exodus: "Pharaoh became afraid and forced them to become slaves." This bridging sentence has effectively skipped the whole story of Joseph but allows you to easily return in the future and say, "Now I'd like to fill in some of the gaps and tell you about Isaac's children and grandchildren and how God protected them in Egypt."

Giving the listeners a feel for the chronology of the Bible communicates God's sovereign control over history. If biblical history and the known history of a culture overlap, then it can be helpful to say, "Today's story happened about the time of X event in your history." This makes the stories more relevant and real.

Ending Well

The goal when ending a story is to finish in such a way that the listener wants to hear the next story. A friend of mine in the Philippines suggests finishing each story the way soap operas conclude on television—essentially saying, "More next time," or "To be continued." Television shows and serialized movies tend to end with a cliffhanger, leaving us in suspense wondering what will happen next. This is an excellent way to end Bible stories if at all possible. This method taps into popular culture and is widely understood. Sometimes we can simply conclude with, "I'll tell you more next time about the coming Savior."

Suspense is an important tool that keeps people pondering a story and wanting to hear the next episode. Sometimes we are tempted to end their suspense, but if we do, we ruin the story. Mr. and Mrs. Lim sell handbags and luggage a few times a week on the side of the road. After I told them the crucifixion story they begged to know, "But does Jesus rise from the dead?" I smiled and said, "I'll tell you next time!" They were really ready to hear the final story, having been in suspense for a whole week.

Another effective way to end is to ask a question that leads into the next story. It could be as simple as, "I wonder what will happen next?" Or it can be a question related to the content of the next story. For example, the creation story could be concluded with, "At the beginning God declared that the world was 'very good.' Is it still like that?" Then, after they've answered, say, "The next story will explain what went wrong." Or, to end the Old Testament stories, you could say, "Faithful people had been waiting for the Savior for thousands of years. When would he come? Who would he be? How would he save us?"

Using Gestures

Ong emphasizes the importance of gestures in storytelling. He notes that even when we are totally immobile, our gestures are communicating something.[3] For example, motionlessness might suggest we are bored with a story. However, at the appropriate time—perhaps as Jesus is buried—it might communicate grief and disappointment, especially if accompanied by slower than normal speaking speed. Gestures are influenced by culture, gender and lots of other factors. How many times have I found myself on home assignment in Australia using the Taiwanese hand gestures for the numbers six and ten and for death? They are totally incomprehensible in Australia.

One reason for not using pictures or memorization in story-telling is that it allows us to be more relaxed in our gestures. Good storytellers don't use huge numbers of gestures, but the ones they do use are relaxed and powerful. You will probably find yourself increasingly acting in your storytelling. For example, you might hang your head as you tell of Adam and Eve emerging from behind the tree to talk to God. Your face will show the emotion of the story. Those with a background in acting or dance will find they have some advantages in storying. Video-recording our storytelling can help us notice whether our gestures enhance or detract from the story. We can also ask a friend to listen in and note what we're doing at each point, along with how it impacts the story experience.

Using Voice

Our voice is one of the key components of an interesting story. Have you ever endured a story told in a monotone voice? It can destroy the best of stories. However, if we can learn to use the whole range of our voice, listeners will be riveted. If the story includes people shouting, then shout! For example, Goliath shouted his challenge to the Israelite army in 1 Samuel 17. What would his voice have been like? Try to make your voice like his—deep and rough and *loud*! In contrast, David was still a teenager and when Goliath heard him he was not impressed. Perhaps his voice was still breaking and sounded very nonthreatening. Go through your story and think about the voice of each character. Practice their lines in the story out loud on the basis of your reflection.

To Use Pictures or Not?

How often have we heard the adage, "A picture is worth a thousand words"? When I first started storying I used a set of pictures. My local friends (new believers) were keen to use them. However, we quickly discovered that the pictures were a problem. They inhibited the storytelling in many ways. The listener became focused on the pictures rather than the story and as a result remembered less. Sometimes the listener wanted to discuss the picture rather than the story—this problem tends to increase the further removed from the local culture the pictures are. Also, the storyteller tended to rely on the pictures to remind him or her what was next in the story. If there wasn't a picture for every section of the story, the storyteller would just skip that section and then get flustered after realizing what he or she had done. And, finally, physically holding the pictures and turning them over inhibited the storyteller's normal gestures and made him or her appear stiff and unnatural.

In the end I've totally abandoned pictures except for one: a picture of the tabernacle. Dale Jones, who works in Cambodia, says, "Pictures are not necessary and can even bring confusion. . . . How can we be sure that our pictures are communicating the right message? . . . The communicator who is armed with nothing but what he carries along with him in his heart is never hindered from sharing just because he doesn't have [pictures or visual aids]."[4] IMB missionaries Rob and Donna also discovered that pictures can be a hindrance rather than a help:

> One of our early experiences was with a man, Tom, who was a nonreader, elderly, and lived alone. We met him out in the community and became friends. We began storying with him and he was very animated, but quickly it became obvious that his worldview was different. Our local coworker began with Genesis and God creating the world. We also used large pictures, which he seemed to like.
>
> After the story, Tom let us know that he already knew about this story. He said it was the story of reincarnation and the animals reflected that. No matter what the storyteller said, Tom was convinced of his own interpretation. He was also bothered that there was only one bird in the picture; he said there should have been two. A lot of superstition and fear surrounded his thinking as we storied with him. We had previously heard that pictures can distract people. Now we experienced it. Images, symbols and pictures are not always easy for people to interpret.[5]

One situation in which pictures might be helpful is in attracting a crowd. This is most effective if an artist draws the picture on the spot. Rob and Donna later used this approach in an earthquake disaster area. Rob drew stick figures and found that these pictures were less distracting. They also signaled that a story was about to begin.

Using Symbols

A Singaporean missionary working in a women's prison is experimenting with using symbols to represent each story in a set. The symbol functions as a memory prompt.[6] When the group developed their initial set of stories, they came up with a symbol to represent each story, which enabled the women to remember the whole set. In another context they used a crown to tell a whole series of stories about Jesus as king. This crown became a crown of thorns when they shared how King Jesus died for them. These symbols might act not just as a memory prompt or theme but also as a tool for reflection and application. For example, which kind of crown would we prefer and why? What can we learn from Jesus' example in facing suffering?

Many objects in the Old Testament functioned as symbols reminding the Israelites of their history. For example, eating the bitter herbs and lamb reminded them of the bitterness of their slavery in Egypt and how God rescued them. On the Day of Atonement, white clothing represented the holiness needed to approach God. The curtain separating off the holy of holies emphasized the vast chasm between a holy God and an unholy people. These rituals and festivals reminded the Israelites of the truth before they had access to the Scriptures.

Jesus himself taught using powerful metaphors that could be considered symbols. For example, Jesus says, "I am the good shepherd. The good shepherd lays down his life for his sheep" (Jn 10:11). This terminology would have immediately reminded his listeners of David, who was a shepherd of literal sheep but became a shepherd of his people. An astute listener would also remember the words of Ezekiel, who condemned Israel's leaders as self-centered shepherds who exploited the flock (Ezek 34). This metaphor reminds us of God's care for us and accompanying presence throughout our spiritual journey (Ps 23). A shepherd's crook or another shepherding symbol could be chosen to represent this metaphor. It could be linked with a powerful story series on David, on those who were good or bad shepherds, or on how Jesus laid down his life for the sheep. Another metaphor Jesus uses is the "living water" (Jn 4:10) that quenches thirst eternally. This metaphor is explicitly linked with the story of the woman of Samaria but could also be used to tell stories of other people who were spiritually thirsty and how Jesus met their thirst.

How Does the Surrounding Culture Tell Stories?

This is really a question for those working crossculturally and was pointed out to me by an experienced storyteller.[7] Different cultures tell stories differently. The closer a storyteller is to her own culture, the more likely she is to tell the story in a culturally sensitive way. This includes consideration of such things as:

- Use of repetition and emphasis.

- Use of humor. Anyone who has ever tried to tell a joke in a crosscultural situation will know that many fail completely.

- How they start stories. If people in the culture habitually start a story with a proverb, you'll have to become a collector of proverbs and learn how to apply them to spiritual situations.

- Where they put the climax of the story. The Bible may put the climax or important teaching point in the center to emphasize it. For example, the point of hope in the Genesis 3 story is in the center (verse 15). In the David and Goliath story the hint that unlocks the meaning of the whole story is found in the middle of David's encounter with Goliath, when David says, "You come against me with sword and spear and javelin, but I come against you in the name of the Lord Almighty, the God of the armies of Israel, whom you have defied. This day the Lord will hand you over to me . . . and the whole world will know that there is a God in Israel. All those gathered here will know that it is not by sword or spear that the Lord saves; for the battle is the Lord's" (1 Sam 17:45-47). Most Western stories place the climax about ninety percent of the way through the story. In certain cultures if we did that, the listeners would not notice it.

It will help if we listen to as many traditional stories as possible. We can also take note of traditional art forms like music, drama, poetry and puppetry and how believers in the culture tell Bible stories. Usually there is someone in the culture who can be a valuable resource to aid our learning.

Preparing a Set of Stories

For your first effort, choose something easy, with between four and eight stories in the set. Read the whole text in the Bible at least three times. Then choose the story sections you want to include, making sure your choices don't skew the story. For example, I have heard many versions of the Abraham story. The problem with nearly all of them is that only Abraham's good points are revealed and he ends up sounding like a perfect man. The story ends up supporting the common "brick" that being a believer is all about being "good." But if the story of Hagar is included, you suddenly have someone who doesn't trust God, takes a mistress and then allows her and her son to be abused. There are actually more stories about Abraham's lack of faith than about his faith. When these failures are included in our stories, it becomes a miracle of God's grace that Abraham was chosen and named "father of faith."

Once you have your single stories selected, work out how to build a bridge between the stories. This might be as simple as saying, "There's still another story." Another method is to mention the passing of time: "Many years passed," or "Noah's sons had sons and they had sons for many generations." Or it can be slightly more complex—for example, prior to the Daniel 4 story: "Many years passed and Nebuchadnezzar had probably been king for at least thirty years when this incident happened. This king reigned from 603 to 562 B.C. and the stories in Daniel stretch from the beginning to the end of his reign." Finally, get out and practice and then polish and evaluate, continually improving your stories and delivery.

Storying a Whole Book of the Bible

The steps are the same as above. The key question to ask yourself is how many stories you should include in the set. With experience you'll begin to work out how many stories people can listen to before wanting a change. You can then design your series to contain fewer stories than this number. That is, we want to conclude a series *before* we bore people, while they're still interested. Like running a Bible study series, you can divide a long book up into sections and insert different story sets in between. You might tell eight 1 Samuel stories, go to a New Testament set, and then return and do a second section from 1 Samuel.

My first set of stories was a basic evangelism set. I used these exclusively for almost four years before I started devising other sets. It took this long for me to learn about storying and become comfortable with the whole method. The people I was working with needed to hear that set first, and I didn't have the energy to devise new ones. Plus, I hadn't yet learned how to use storying in the context of discipleship or Bible study groups. Somewhere during this time I started experimenting with a series of six stories on Daniel. This was my second set simply because I'd spoken at a conference on Daniel and Nebuchadnezzar and so had done the prework. The set came together easily. Later for another conference I learned a series of stories on Elijah.

I'm now in a cultural context where many nonbelievers are hearing stories but they are not ready to become Christians after hearing the first set. This has pushed me to develop other sets. I've done two or three stories on Jonah, three on Joseph, a set on 1 Samuel, a set on parables and stories on Acts. Each set becomes easier to learn. By and large a new set is the result of either my spiritual journey, what God has brought to my attention or the result of the demands or needs of listeners.

Action

1. Spend time praying first about your preparation and choice of story.

2. Choose the first Bible story in your set and start the process above. Remember not to write the stories down. Do it orally. If you write the story down it will change how it sounds. Audio- or video-record your completed stories if necessary.

3. Think about your stories. What gestures could you add or delete to help your communication?

4. Do you agree with this chapter's conclusions about using pictures? Why or why not? How will you prove or disprove your current thinking?

5. If you are in a crosscultural context, what do you learn listening to the local stories? What adaptations could you make to your stories based on this learning?

PART THREE

SOW AND TELL: Getting Out and Using Storying

GETTING STARTED

Agroup of fifteen elders and deacons at a church in rural Taiwan had requested training in storying. I invested many months training them for one evening every other week. They learned the stories thoroughly and were better storytellers than I. However, in the end few of them actually went out and used the stories. There were many reasons for this, including an inexperienced trainer, but the point is that unless we go out and tell stories, it doesn't matter how many we learn. The stories only sink into the teller's heart when we get out and share them. The purpose is to sow the gospel seed widely, and to do this, not surprisingly, we actually have to tell the stories.

Basic Evangelism Principles

Storytelling is only one method of evangelism and, as such, the basic principles of evangelism still apply. Here they are.

Pray, pray, pray. Evangelism of any sort relies one hundred percent on God. His Spirit supplies the motivation to share and all the resources we need to do so. No matter how good our method is, there are no shortcuts to fervent, constant prayer. Forgetting this principle will cut us off from our source of wisdom and power.

We need to pray for people's hearts to be opened and prepared for the good news (see Col 4:3-4). We need to pray for personal boldness as Paul did (Eph 6:19). Throughout our storytelling we need to keep praying and asking God for his help to apply it into people's lives.

Remember that success is not method-based. Look at Jonah, one of the worst missionaries in history. He wanted God to judge those he was preaching to, not forgive them. He hoped no one would listen to his message or repent. Yet his tiny sermon succeeded because God chose to raise the spiritually dead.

Having said that, there's no excuse for a poor method, and Bible storying lays a strong foundation for people to understand the gospel and grow. If we are to avoid stress in sharing our faith with others, it is important that we be clear on what is our part and what is God's part. Look at Colossians 4:2-6 and 1 Peter 3:15-16. What is our part in evangelism?

In Ephesians 2:1 Paul says that nonbelievers are "dead in [their] transgressions and sins." He knows the limitations of human abilities and that no one is able to raise the dead except God. Understanding this brings us tremendous freedom. We are free to share the gospel knowing *the results are up to God.*

Paul makes the same point in 1 Corinthians 3. When he wrote this letter, the Corinthian believers were playing power games by claiming to follow different religious leaders. Paul exposes their wrong thinking and says, "What, after all, is Apollos? And what is Paul? Only servants, through whom you came to believe—as the Lord has assigned to each his task. I planted the seed, Apollos watered it, but God made it grow. So neither he who plants nor he who waters is anything, but only God, who makes things grow" (1 Cor 3:5-7).

Although I personally believe that storying is one of the best and perhaps *the* best way to do evangelism, we must not forget the implications of Ephesians 2:1. No matter what method we use, *not one guarantees one hundred percent success.* No matter how clear our presentation of the gospel, people are still dead and don't want to hear it. So let go of unrealistic expectations. Jesus was the best communicator in history and also had the advantage of knowing people's thoughts, and yet he didn't have widespread initial success. In fact, he suffered the ultimate rejection of his message: crucifixion.

Never stop learning. Every year we should improve in our ability to relate to people—both in depth and in the kinds of people we communicate with. We should also keep improving in our ability to communicate truth simply and clearly. This doesn't happen by accident. If we continually ask, "Lord, how can I improve?" God will be delighted to show us.

Be wise. Sometimes say nothing. There are times in evangelism when it is best to say nothing at all. Just be there to listen or serve rather than speak. This can communicate Jesus' love and prepare people's hearts to listen to stories later. We need to be aware of the larger picture, which includes service, prayer and testimony as components of evangelism. Rushing in too early with words in certain contexts can wreck relationships. The Holy Spirit is more than able to let us know when the time to speak has come.

Recently, May's fifty-five-year-old husband died from liver cancer. I went to the funeral and just listened and supported her the first two months. I kept praying for the Holy Spirit to prepare her heart and tell me when she was ready to start hearing stories. Eventually the opportunity came. So most weeks now I can be spotted standing behind her meat stall between the chopping block and the meat mincer and telling stories to May and her sister as they work.

Another one of my contacts is an ardent Buddhist who reads Buddhist scriptures daily. She has made it abundantly clear that she will never listen to Bible stories and has prevented her husband from doing so, despite his interest. Two years later her attitude is beginning to soften as she has reluctantly come to enjoy my company. It may be years yet before she is ready to hear stories. Other people are ready the first time we meet. The Holy Spirit's discernment is needed to distinguish which kind of person is which.

Ways to Increase Our Likelihood of Using Storying

There are some things we can do to get more comfortable sharing the stories we've taken the time and effort to learn.

Get lots of practice. Most people need to tell each story between ten and twenty times to get it solidly in memory. People lacking confidence may need to practice on their own first. As mentioned earlier, stories should be practiced out loud or we will simply jump over the difficult parts mentally and then stumble over them when we tell the story.

Practice in easy situations first. What's considered "easy" will vary from person to person. Some people are comfortable enough to go out immediately and share with nonbelievers. Others need to practice a few times with other storytellers. Then they need to share with people in their church. This works well if you focus on people who are on the outskirts of the church community. Some of them might actually be nonbelievers or at least be shaky in their understanding of the Bible.

Tanya believed she was a Christian but showed no evidence of new life. If I had suggested to her that she didn't understand salvation, she would have been highly insulted. So I asked if I might share a set of stories with her. She said, "Oh, those are for children. I've been a Christian for fifteen years!"

"Just listen to two stories," I replied. "If you really don't like them, we'll stop."

After the Genesis 3 story, we had a deep discussion about sin. She realized it wasn't just doing "bad things" but wanting to be like God in our hearts—wanting to be king instead of God. Suddenly she said, "I've just realized I'm not a Christian!" She had thought that being a Christian meant trying to be good and going to church meetings.

Even before we reached the New Testament stories it was obvious that Tanya had come to new life. The stories got in under the barriers of pride she'd erected without my having to say anything directly.

Learn to slow down. Jillian was a retired schoolteacher who wanted to be trained to use Bible stories in evangelism. In our first session she confessed, "The biggest barrier for me is that I'm too efficient and task-oriented. I rush to the shops with a list and am only there long enough to do what needs to be done. I need to learn to slow down and work on relationships. Only then will I be able to tell people stories."

Having identified this major issue, we talked about why Jillian rushed everywhere. In a few weeks she began to report that she was having opportunities to share in the market and in small shops. She had to learn, as I have, that people are more important than tasks. She learned to deliberately leave the house earlier for errands so she could spend time talking to people and seize opportunities to tell stories.

Deal with fear. Fear is probably the main reason we don't do storying. In fact, fear is a disease that will stop us from doing many worthwhile things and almost certainly inhibit any kind of evangelism. The wonderful thing is that fear can be overcome. This doesn't mean we won't experience it but that it no longer needs to influence our behavior. Here's what we can do.

Acknowledge the root causes. Satan uses fear as one of his most successful weapons. When we look at what we fear, it's often so petty it's embarrassing. Most of us don't fear what we ought (that we might be bringing God dishonor) but instead fear being laughed at or rejected. Our fear is often self-centered.

Acknowledge any parts of our fear that are sinful. We may find it difficult to admit that a fear is a sin. True, some fears are sensible (we ought to fear dangerous situations, for example), but many times we fear because we don't trust God. We refuse to believe what his Word says. We need to take our fears to the Lord and let him shine his light on them. Under this light, fears will shrink back to their real size—tiny in comparison to our great God.

Choose to trust God's Word. One of our problems in the Christian life is that we look at ourselves far too often and forget to look at Jesus—or choose not to. When he commanded us to go and make disciples of all nations (Mt 28:18-20), he didn't leave us to do it on own. He promised us all the resources of God himself. That means the limiting factor is not us ourselves but our willingness to trust God. It's a choice that will change our lives. God is looking for people to be one hundred percent submitted to him. Won't we choose to be among those people? What prevents us?

Remind ourselves of God's Word. Go through the Bible and write down promises that relate to the area of sharing the gospel and fear. Here are some of my personal favorites:

• Exodus 4. Moses uses the excuse of being a poor communicator to try to avoid being used by God. He is more afraid of failure than of God. God has to rebuke him with the words, "Who made your mouth?" (Ex 4:11). If God made my mouth then he is more than able to help me dare to open it and give me the words I need.

• Hebrews 13:5-8. Jesus has promised us that he will never leave us or forsake us. So we can say with confidence, "The Lord is my helper; I will not be afraid. What can man do to me?" If Jesus, who is the same yesterday, today and forever, helped the apostles in Acts, he can do the same today. If Peter, who denied Jesus after his arrest and showed both fear and a failure to trust, experienced Jesus' gracious forgiveness (Jn 21:15-17) and went on to become a fearless evangelist, the same Holy Spirit can transform us.

• 1 Corinthians 1:27-29. "God chose the weak things of the world to shame the strong . . . so that no one can boast before him." If we think we're weak, then we qualify to be greatly used by God. He gains far more glory from our lives than from the lives of the obviously talented.

When I feel fearful, which is every time I want to tell a story to someone, I immediately remind myself of these verses and then open my mouth. Once I've chosen to obey, the fear flees. Darkness cannot bear the presence of the light.

Transitioning from Ordinary Conversation to a Story

If I were writing about my old style of evangelism before storying, I would have needed a whole book for this topic. It is far easier to introduce storytelling than traditional evangelism openers. For example, you might simply say, "I've been learning to tell stories. The trainer has asked us to practice each story with ten people. Would you be willing to listen to a five-minute story and tell me if you understood it?"

A friend of mine has used this approach: "I love stories. Do you? Could you tell me one and then I'll tell you one?" This works especially well for someone working crossculturally and wanting to hear stories from that culture. This way you can be learning language and culture at the same time as sharing the gospel.

Sue was a new Christian who wondered how God could use her to share stories. She had one skill—hairdressing—and just enough money to rent one room and cut hair. Every time she cut someone's hair, she offered a "free story" as a gift. Many people accepted this bonus offer. Over time she saw numbers of people accepting the greatest gift of all.

Another approach is to establish a reputation as a storyteller. When someone asks, "What do you do?" you could say something like, "I'm a teacher—but what I really love to do is tell stories." Establishing this reputation means you'll seldom have to start a gospel conversation from scratch. People will start asking you for stories. Sometimes this is as easy as carrying a prop with you. I started telling stories in a park and discovered that carrying a small pink plastic stool with me signaled to people that it was story time.

After moving to a new house, Bronwyn went to buy new shower curtains. A saleswoman smiled at her, leading to a brief conversation about Bronwyn's surprising ability to speak Mandarin. "Are you a teacher?" the saleswoman finally asked.

"No, I'm a storyteller," Bronwyn replied. The conversation finished and Bronwyn moved on. A few minutes later the saleswoman came looking for her. She wanted to know where Bronwyn told stories and to whom. Bronwyn explained that the stories were for anyone, at any place; yes, even at McDonald's. "To my excitement, she gave me her name and number so that I could contact her and arrange a time to come and tell stories," Bronwyn reports.

You can also wear something that sparks curiosity. A T-shirt that contains questions, symbols from early stories or a Bible verse might stimulate questions, to which you can reply, "There's a story that goes with this shirt."

I wear a necklace with the Chinese character for "right-eousness." This is an unusual character to wear and I chose it because others, such as "love," are commonly worn by nonbelievers and wouldn't garner much attention. I hoped people would ask me why I wore that character, especially when they realized it was not linked with my Chinese name.

One day I had a meal with a traditional Chinese family at a restaurant. I was seated opposite two women in their twenties at a long table. The younger one asked me why that character was on my necklace. I asked her what she thought the word meant and then told her it was linked to the stories I tell. However, I warned her that a thorough answer would require me to tell a long series of stories because the answer was contained in stories four, five, six and thirteen. I promised to not tell them in their entirety. Intrigued, the girl and her sister listened to the whole basic set. I drew several pictures on my paper placemat. They became animated as they worked out the significance of why Jesus was crucified on Passover and why the temple curtain ripped at his death.

On another occasion I cleared customs too early at the airport and so had to fill in time. I wandered through some of the duty-free shops and a lady at the jewelry counter inquired about my necklace. She and another sales associate listened to my first two stories, then I explained about the lamb and bridged into how Jesus was the lamb who came to "take away the sins of the world" (Jn 1:29). I left them with a small portion of scripture, Genesis

1–4. For my next flight I again arrived early, hoping to follow up. I discovered that these women had told two others, a man and a woman, and they'd all read the Scripture portion. I now have to turn up early each time I fly as there are five people who've heard stories up to the exodus and are waiting to hear more.

Questions are another great way to bridge into stories. For example, ask, "How do you think the world got here?" Listen to the person's point of view (this is essential), then ask if you can tell a story you believe addresses that question. Another easy conversation starter: "Why is the world such a painful place to live in?" Almost everyone has an opinion on that. Listen first to that opinion, then ask if you can tell a story. You can still tell the creation story first by saying, "The world was originally perfect. Can I tell a five-minute story about that first and then explain what went wrong?" Letting people know the length of the stories is useful because it lets them know this won't be an endless conversation from which there is no escape.

Mr. and Mrs. Lim, handbag sellers, had just experienced a natural disaster that buried their hometown in mud twelve feet deep. They shared their grief and pain, which enabled me to ask (very gently), "Why do such terrible things happen?" Their viewpoint was formed by their religious upbringing. They wondered what terrible sin their town and they as individuals had committed to result in this disaster. Our discussion led me to tell the Genesis 1–3 stories. Normally I would tell these in two separate sessions, but that day it was the second part they needed to hear. Rather than skip the creation section, I used it to set up the contrast between the perfect world God created and the current one marred by sin.

Sometimes we find ourselves in a situation where there's no interest in stories. A "pre-story" that keeps some details under wraps might be one way to arouse curiosity. I've just started experimenting with this method with an older couple who are not ready to hear the creation story. Their adult children have heard many stories, but I would like the whole family to listen together in hopes that this extended family might become a new house church.

In Taiwan the seventh lunar month (about August) is "ghost" month. The Taiwanese believe that the spirits of people whose families don't worship them or provide for their needs at this time are released from hell. During ghost month families need to make three offerings at specific times and follow certain rituals. One evening during ghost month I told a story at a crowded meal table. Before the story I asked, "What do the Taiwanese fear?" My dinner companions mentioned ghosts and spirits, graveyards, the dark and death. I asked about ghost month and why they made their offerings. Did they truly believe in ghosts or were they just following a tradition? Some of the family really seemed to believe in ghosts, while younger members just did the rituals to keep their elders happy. After listening to their responses, I told this story:

> Two thousand years ago there lived a man who terrified his neighbors. He was possessed by a group of ghosts, or evil spirits. He lived in the local graveyard next to the sea, and was so wild that he didn't wear clothes, he cut himself, and he often cried out in a loud voice. The local people tried to restrain him with chains, but the spirits made him so strong that he just snapped those.
>
> One day a boat drew up to the shore next to the graveyard. A man got out and twelve others followed him. When the spirit-possessed man saw the first man, he ran and fell to his knees in front of him and said, "What do you want with me, son of the most high God? Swear to God that you won't torture me!" For the man from the boat had already told the spirits to leave. The spirits begged the man not to send them into the abyss. Instead, they asked permission to go into a large herd of pigs. They did and were drowned.
>
> The pig herders ran into the local town and told everyone what had happened. The people came to see, and right away

they noticed the man dressed and in his right mind sitting at the stranger's feet. The people were afraid and they asked the stranger to leave. The freed man begged to go with go with the men in the boat, but he was told, "Return home and tell how much God has done for you." So that is what the man did.

Originally I told the story with Jesus' name included, but now think it would have been better to be vague and ask, "Who was this stranger who had such power?" I concluded by saying, "This story comes from a book of stories. It's toward the end. I'd love to tell you stories from the beginning and then tell you more about this man."

The town where I live is a fishing port. My coworker and I spend time each week walking and praying for our town street by street. We've met several groups of fishermen chatting and drinking tea. I think telling a few of the Bible's fishing stories would lead to interest in hearing more. I could perhaps tell these as "fish stories," such as, "Have you heard the one about a man who lived three days in the belly of a fish?" Or, "Have you heard the story about the men who caught so many fish that their boat nearly sank?" Or, "Did you hear about the fisherman who walked on water?" Pre-stories could be selected to communicate with farmers, business people, medics, prostitutes and tax collectors.

Though you might think finding an opening for stories is difficult at first, it becomes easier with practice and as God gives you confidence. Lynne recalls her early experiences of telling stories in Central Asia:

> Over the last four years I have sat at an uncountable number of local parties, and each of them was the same. We would sit on the floor around a tablecloth filled with bread and sweets, about twenty ladies in the room, and the ladies would gossip while I would sit there silent and frustrated, wishing I could share something that would lead them to know the Lord but not knowing where to begin. Starting is always the hardest, isn't it?

Then as I began to grow in confidence telling the creation and Fall stories to individual women, I started to realize that there are opportunities to begin all over the place. The more I would tell the stories, the more links and ways to begin I would see. I also noticed that the Lord was prompting me and I was often just too fearful to open my mouth. By the time I got up the courage, the conversation would have moved on. I determined that, with the Lord's help, I would try to act immediately on any idea he gave me.

Surprise, surprise, at the very next party I went to, a lady had come back from years living as a "foreigner" and "stranger" in Russia and spoke of how hard it was. They all turned to me and commiserated with me that I was also away from my homeland. There was my opportunity! "But I hope you realize that I'm not the only foreigner here," I said. "Actually we are all foreigners, away from our true homeland because none of us are in the special place God created for us. Let me tell you a story from the holy book . . . "

When You've Finished the Basic Set of Stories

Rob met Andrew and Jo on the streets of Sydney and showed strong interest in hearing stories. Andrew and Jo suggested that Rob bring a couple of friends to come hear a first story. This initial event grew into a weekly gathering. After the second week and the story of Adam and Eve's rebellion against God (Gen 3), Rob made a thoughtful comment: "Oh, now I understand. Sin and death are separation from God." He began to grasp that people have a serious problem. Adam and Eve's rebellion was not about casually eating a piece of fruit but about disregarding God's word, rejecting his authority and setting themselves up in opposition to him.

The group continued through more Old Testament stories and then moved on to stories of Jesus. One of the gatherings involved a deep discussion on why Jesus wept just before raising Lazarus from the dead (Jn 11). Little did the group know the impact this was about to have. Rob abruptly let the group know he was moving to Melbourne, which meant this last session suddenly had to cover Jesus' death, resurrection and ascension. Halfway through the discussion time, Rob burst into tears. A university friend had died of cancer the night before; she was twenty-five. After the Lazarus story had opened the door to a discussion of grief and death, the group was able to talk deeply about resurrection, hope and salvation. Rob became a Christian that night.

This is the kind of story we hope for. We would love for all of our hearers to listen to a series of stories, recognize the implications and become Christians at the end. I have to admit that I seldom experience this. Most of the people I work with have no biblical background. A set of fourteen stories is not enough time or information for them to commit their lives to Jesus. So what do we do when we finish a series of stories and our listener hasn't come to believe?

One possibility is to create a longer series of stories to allow more time. I've personally resisted this option because I want a reasonable-length basic set that allows me to complete the stories with the maximum number of people. Also, as the set gets longer it becomes increasingly difficult to train people. They become overwhelmed by the thought of learning so many stories. A better solution is to use follow-up stories or other forms of follow-up. Here are some suggestions for what to do after the basic set.

Cease storying. Ask your listeners what they want to do next. Let them know you'd be delighted to tell more stories, but if they want to stop, that's their choice. If this is what they choose, let them know they can always change their mind—they just need to ask. This relaxed freedom is very important. First of all, we don't want to be telling stories to people who don't want to listen. Second, we don't want people to feel pressure to hear the gospel. If they feel obligated to us or embarrassed to refuse, or if we use manipulation (certain people are more prone to this), then we undermine our purpose. The best path is to pray that our hearers will feel internal pressure from the Holy Spirit so they become spiritually hungry and seek us out in order to know more.

It's important to communicate that our friendship isn't based on whether they choose to follow Jesus or not. It is bad testimony when people believe we care about them only if they're listening to stories. Make a point to continue spending time with people even if they don't want to hear any more stories, and keep praying that the stories will penetrate their hearts. One of the reasons I like to have a complete, shorter basic set is that even if people choose to cease hearing stories, the ones they've heard will have adequately explained our problem and God's amazing solution. The stories will keep working in their hearts whether they see us frequently or not.

Mrs. Wong was in her sixties and sold peanuts on the side of the road. She listened enthusiastically to the stories that led up to Jesus' death. We had deep discussions along the way. Suddenly she seemed to realize that Jesus' death had implications for her life. She began to count the cost and decided that she wasn't willing to pay it. What had been an open door suddenly became closed. She allowed me to complete the set but asked not to hear further sets. I continue to pray for her heart to be open again but remain confident that the Spirit will continue to work through the stories she has heard so far. This situation is a win-win. Mrs. Wong has heard a complete set and I am free to share with others who are more open at present. It would be distressing and counterproductive to be storying with someone who had closed their ears and heart.

Watch the Jesus film or an equivalent. The Jesus film is a powerful conclusion to the first story set.[1] It is available in multiple languages on one DVD and is cheap to buy—so cheap, in fact, that I once gave one away on a bus to a young working-class man who had responded well to the first two stories and whom I was unlikely to meet again. You can watch the Jesus film in three or four sections or all in one sitting. Ask your listeners which they'd prefer. It works best if you watch it with them. That way they can ask questions. Certain kinds of people will ask questions throughout and you'll have to keep hitting the pause button.

Tell more stories. It doesn't really matter what set of stories you do next. Seize the opportunity to prepare a new set if you don't have one ready. You could tell more stories of Jesus, perhaps ten more miracle stories or ten parables or stories that deal directly with the "bricks" in your listener's worldview. I'm presently starting a set on Joseph with two people who have heard the basic set, Elijah, Daniel and Acts and still aren't ready to follow Jesus. Why do I persist with them? My principle is, "While they're willing to hear, keep going!" I also deliberately leave periods of time (perhaps four weeks) when I only drop in and chat and don't tell stories. I pray that they miss hearing stories and so develop a hunger to hear more.

Tell stories leading to response and baptism. At some point (after you've prayed about it) you might begin to tell stories that challenge the listener to think about accepting Jesus' offer of salvation and being baptized. J. O. Terry suggests using the parable of the wedding banquet (Mt 22:1-14).[2] It's natural in the discussion afterward to talk about the kind of excuses people can make in response to God's invitation. However, I've found in my situation that it's necessary to tell other parables first because my working-class Taiwanese friends aren't used to interpreting stories with hidden meanings.

Another suggestion from Terry is to tell a series of stories from the beginning of Acts. These stories naturally emphasize that baptism is the way people express their commitment to following Jesus. The hope is that the listener will say, "I want to be baptized too." I'm doing this at the moment with Mr. and Mrs. Lim. At first they didn't seem to notice the constant mentions of baptism. But after the story of the Ethiopian eunuch in Acts 8, they suddenly asked, "Do we have to be baptized to follow Jesus?" We had a fantastic conversation in which I asked them questions rather than telling them answers, and they seemed to work through many issues.

Do a Bible study. My goal is always that people read the Bible for themselves or hear it if they can't read. And one way for that to happen is through a more structured Bible study. I strongly recommend doing initial Bible studies from the biblical narrative. In 2009, I was asked to start a Bible study group at a church with 250 attendees. This church had had no Bible study groups for more than twenty years. The congregation was dubious about trying storying and various members felt that telling Bible stories was demeaning to them. So we compromised. First I would tell the story, and then we'd do a short Bible study on an aspect of it. This worked well.

Do whatever God leads you to do! If we're doing Bible storying it is never a waste of time. Stories are so powerful that they will have an impact on people's lives now or decades into the future. It's wonderful to have the opportunity to share a whole set with someone but even better to share more. Lynne reflects more of her early storying experiences:

> Two things had really been holding me back from storying more widely and more often. The first was that as a woman I felt I should not share stories with men. There were many reasons for this: my church background, which is strongly against women teaching men, an assumption that my message would be ignored because in this [Muslim] culture men do not normally take advice from women, and so on. The second barrier was that I felt embarrassed to retell a story in front of someone who had already heard it. My Westerner's brain reasoned that it would be boring for them to hear it over again.
>
> Long taxi drives are wonderful places to practice telling stories. The passengers are bored and the driver likes anything that helps keep him awake. So on a long and dusty trip

to the capital city, over two mountain passes with perilous drop-offs littered with car corpses, I began telling my first few stories to a local friend I was traveling with. I needed the practice and she desperately needed something to take her mind off how carsick she felt. The stories were rough-and-ready—but all the people in the jeep listened in.

A week later was the return journey, with the same friend and same driver and two new passengers. One of the new passengers, a man, was intrigued by something I said, and when I said it was explained in a story, he pressed me to tell it. But the driver and my friend had heard before! And two of the listeners were men! God was about to change my assumptions and free me from lies that were stopping his word from going out.

So I told the first two stories. I have never had a car full of people so engaged. The taxi driver even began to help me to tell the story. Although my language was understandable, he began to throw in idioms and jokes that really made the story come alive in their language.

Reflection

1. Can you think of any other basic evangelism principles not mentioned in this chapter?

2. Which principles do you struggle with? Why?

3. What needs to change in your life so that you can prioritize people and focus on evangelism?

4. What do you fear most in evangelism? What words in Scripture would speak directly to these fears?

5. What method for sharing the first story appeals most to you? What other ideas do you have?

6. Can you think of some intriguing T-shirt designs? Please add any ideas you have to the website linked with this book, <storyingthescriptures.com> (see appendix D).

7. Go out and try telling a story you've learned to five to ten people. Rate your experiences as:

   a. Positive: The person was interested.
   b. Neutral: The person listened but didn't interact or ask questions.
   c. Negative: The person became angry or asked not to hear any more stories.

   What did God teach you from your storying experiences?

8. What are good indicators for continuing with a set of follow-up stories? What might be indicators you should stop storying?

9. Choose the stories for two possible follow-up sets with four to ten stories per set.

LEADING DISCUSSION

The Why and the How

Ruth is a young mother assisting in leading a Bible study group in a church in Sydney, Australia. The church is in a majority migrant area with people of Orthodox (Greek and Russian), Roman Catholic, Muslim and Buddhist backgrounds. Ruth and the other leaders have faithfully led traditional kinds of Bible studies for years but have struggled. Many of the group participants have low levels of English and there is often a deafening silence when they attempt any kind of discussion. Is it because the participants simply don't understand what's going on? Are the questions too abstract? Are there other reasons they haven't even thought of?

One evening over dinner Ruth heard the story of the two thieves crucified next to Jesus (Lk 23:39-43) and a style of discussion that was new to her. She personally found the storying and discussion style stimulating and thought it might work in her context. She immediately started experimenting with her Bible study group. She noticed that not only did people seem to pay more attention to the story but that discussion was noticeably improved. At the second week's study one particularly shy woman with poor English told the creation story in front of the whole group.

Leading group discussion is a skill that grows with time. In this chapter we'll explore many different methods you can use to enhance discussions in your own storying. The list of tools is long, but don't panic. It's long because I'm seeking to be comprehensive. Once you get started you'll realize that although there is plenty to learn of this art, anyone can get started.

Why Have Discussion at All?

This question is worth considering. Can't we simply tell the stories? With certain rare individuals, that's all we'll do. But in most cases, discussion has great benefits. Here are its advantages.

Ensures that people remember the stories. This is perhaps the most important benefit of holding a discussion after you tell a story. It's hard to forget a story when you've discussed it and wrestled with its meaning and relevance. Mr. Lin sells roasted sweet potatoes on the side of the road. When I was using storying with him, sometimes he had only a few customers, so there was time for discussion. Other times he was busy and we had to forgo the dialogue afterward. It was obvious which weeks we had discussion because those were the stories he remembered most clearly.

Gives insight into spiritual diagnosis. When we hold discussions, we will start to be able to work out where people are on their "chain" diagram. If we're alert we should also begin discovering the "bricks" (misunderstandings) in their worldview. Listening closely will enable us to learn much about how they think and perhaps see what stories they need to hear. It will also encourage us as we see the Holy Spirit revealing truth to them.

Lets listeners see the relevance to their lives. Although the Holy Spirit is perfectly able to apply a story into someone's life without any discussion, this process seems to be enhanced when discussion does occur. Plus, we get to hear about what the person is thinking.

Stimulates curiosity and spiritual hunger. One of the problems the church has struggled with in the West is the perception that Christianity is anti-intellectual and doesn't encourage questions.

Simply having discussion time helps destroy this myth. In both a Western and non-Western context, discussion makes people think and question their own beliefs. It can show them the weaknesses in their outlook and help them realize their own spiritual emptiness. If the storying is done in a group context, other people's questions can stimulate our own thinking.

Increases the likelihood of wanting to delve into the Bible further. Good discussion will often prompt people to want to read the Bible. You could say something like, "This story is found in Genesis 12–24. There are more details and parts of this story that you haven't heard." Reading the story in the Bible after hearing it cements the story in people's minds and helps them remember more details. In addition, it allows them to compare our story with the Bible. This is a safeguard for us because they won't usually hesitate to tell us if we've been inaccurate. I was delighted one Sunday when I was publically corrected on a story detail in a house church. One of the women knew her Bible better than I did. Storying encourages people to care about accuracy and to correct each other within the group. Plus, our response to comments models how to handle criticism and underlines that the Bible is the authority and standard for our stories.

Grows relationships. If we only told stories and then left, we would be regarded as "teachers" or "storytellers" and nothing else. Discussion leads to mutual learning. It shows that we don't know it all and are ourselves still in the process of learning from the Bible. As we discuss stories, we are far more likely to be viewed as ordinary people who are on a journey to discover truth. This is turn leads to the next benefit.

Starts to create a sense of gathering. For my first five years of telling stories I tended to work more one-to-one or with pairs. Recently I've started purposely attempting to gather groups to hear stories. This can help people in the group transition into a small group or house church. This is particularly relevant if we're aiming to start churches led by working-class people themselves rather than someone they see as more "able" or "educated."

You could form this type of gathering by asking an interested person whether he or she has other friends and family they could invite along to hear the stories. There are myriad ways of doing this. You could attend a party or instigate one, then tell a party story from a Gospel to introduce the idea of storytelling. One possibility is the prodigal son story from Luke 15, which ends with a party. This might be a good time to include pre-story questions to prepare the way—for example, "Why do people have parties? . . . This story contains an unusual reason for a party."

Other "party" stories include Levi's dinner party (Mt 9:9-11), Zacchaeus's encounter with Jesus (Lk 19:1-10), Simon the Pharisee's gathering (Lk 7:36-50), the banquet parables (Mt 22:1-14; 25:1-13; Lk 14:15-24) and of course the wedding at Cana (Jn 2). If you're using the story for pre-evangelism and as an advertisement for future stories, make it intriguing and leave it unresolved. You could ask at the end, "Why does God value such strange guests?" Or, "How do you get an invitation to God's party?" Then let people know you love telling stories and if they'd like to hear more you'll regularly share them at a certain time and place. Let them know what kinds of questions the story series will answer. Make the issues relevant to their daily lives.

Stories can be told in any gathering for clubs, sports or hobbies. Alan is interested in model railways and wants to use them for God's glory. He could use "journey" and "railway" themes such as keeping on the tracks or getting to the proper destination as concepts to introduce Bible stories. There are plenty of stories that tell of people going off track. What makes the difference between people that continue off track and those who come back on track?

At its most basic, a church is a gathering of people who worship God in community and encourage one another to know the Lord and mature in him. I long to see every little story group grow from an individual or couple to a community of their friends and family. Quite often by the time we've heard a story and discussed it, we've spent thirty to sixty minutes together. When I sense that people are ready, I teach them to pray, so the meeting becomes word plus discussion plus prayer. Music, drama and song can also be added. As the members of the group become believers, we start praying for their family and friends. They also start to share their testimonies. The hope is that they'll eventually be trained to tell stories themselves.

Look for places where groups gather—old people chatting in a park in the evening or neighbors on the side of the road. Sadly, in modern Taiwan, too few of these gatherings happen. Instead people watch television. It takes time to persuade people to come to a storytelling group rather than watch television. But it's worth the effort because of the special dynamics of group learning. A group storytelling situation is often far more stimulating than one-to-one conversation. It's exciting to hear group members talking around the storyteller, asking new questions or answering each other's questions.

Underlines that questions are acceptable. It's normal for people to have questions and doubts, but they need to feel safe before they'll ask or share. Having a regular time of discussion allows people to grow in their feeling of safety and become comfortable asking their major questions.

Shows that the Bible stands up to scrutiny and convinces people of its relevance and reality. I've found that the first few stories can feel a little distant to people but during the Abraham story they begin to say, "That family is like mine." Once people identify with the characters, they start to become drawn in to the story and more convinced of its truth.

Kinds of Discussion Questions

Discussion questions can be divided up into these categories, although there is a good deal of overlap.

Questions that help build trust. These kinds of questions are designed to be used after you've told the first story. Not everyone is comfortable with discussion—some people need to know they won't be rejected, ridiculed or made to feel stupid. So these first few questions[1] are designed to ease people into the concept of discussion. Generally a person's desire to discuss the story grows, so within in a few stories the discussion takes longer than the story. Here are two questions that are fun to start with and help you check how someone responds to discussion.

"When I talked about X, what did you 'see' in your mind?" After the creation story I often ask, "When I mentioned the birds, which birds did you think of?" I then ask this about the plants, fish and animals. This question is interesting because it validates the hearers' imagination and encourages them to allow it to work. Much modern education (especially in non-Western countries) stifles imagination. Give people permission to see.

It never ceases to amaze me the range of birds people "see." Talking about categories rather than specific species will allow people to "see" in a culturally appropriate way. For example, I often mention flightless birds. I see a kiwi or an emu since I come from those cultural backgrounds. Others see a chicken. For birds that sing beautifully, I see a lyrebird or nightingale. Taiwanese people don't. Many of them have never heard of these birds. Likewise, Africans will "see" their own animals and South Americans something different altogether.

This question's advantage is that there is no right or wrong answer. Even if someone saw nothing, that's not too terrible! The listeners are able to gain confidence just talking and responding in a nonthreatening environment.

Later on in the series of stories, this kind of exercise can be used again. You can ask people to imagine what a certain person looked like. For example, ask them what they thought Jesus looked like. This can be informative because they might focus (as the Bible does) more on his character and say, "kind," "gentle" or "strong." Or they might say something like, "blond with blue eyes and a beard." This reveals something about their misconceptions—a helpful insight, especially in a country that thinks Christianity is a Western religion. You can then initiate a discussion of the fact that Jesus was a Middle Easterner and what this means. In fact, a Western cultural appearance is about the furthest from what figures in the Bible (especially the Old Testament) actually looked like. You could also discuss the fact that the Bible never mentions a single physical characteristic of Jesus, only that "he had no beauty or majesty to attract us to him" (Is 53:2).

"What is your favorite part of the story? Why?" Once again this question doesn't have a right or wrong answer. It is designed to build confidence and can be used repeatedly for people who don't like to discuss. Sometimes they will suddenly ask a question, and a discussion is born.

If your group can't answer the "why" bit of the question, don't worry. Just let them out of it easily so they don't feel like a failure. You'll probably also hear, "I just like it." That's okay. They will likely go home continuing to think about the "why." However, the answers to this question may surprise you. Here are some of the answers I've heard:

- "Noah kept making the boat no matter how much his neighbors laughed. I like this bit because I struggle with persevering when I'm laughed at."
- "God's compassion in saving Noah and his family."
- "I liked the part about God's judgment on the people of Noah's day. The world is a wicked place and it is good to know that God will judge."
- "I like the funny picture of a pregnant ninety-year-old [Sarah]. If God can do that, then he's very powerful."
- "Jesus staying on the cross not because of the nails but because he loved me and wanted to save me."
- "Jesus' compassion on people."
- "The story talks about Peter's failures. These people are just like me."

I sometimes get tears in my eyes hearing people's response to this pair of questions. Their answers can reveal what they're thinking and how they're beginning to apply the story to their life.

Questions that help us notice the content of the story. These questions help people review what they've heard. They also begin to show the stories' relevance and application to life. These kinds of questions work well when you want the group to practice the story together and then individually. You can ask them in a series, such as, "Where was Jesus?" "What did he say to the blind man?" "How did he respond?" Review questions can also be used with young children or a group that's not ready for the more difficult "how" or "why" discussions.

Questions that help us apply the story. As a story set proceeds, our questions should help people identify with the story and apply it to their lives. The more they feel a connection between themselves and the characters, the more real the story will become to them. Application questions are easier to do with Christians, but they are possible with non-Christians too. Here are some examples:

- "How easy is it for us to continue doing something when others laugh at us like the people laughed at Noah? What helps us persevere?"

- "Have you had an experience of failing to trust God like Abraham did? Why? And what was the result?" It's also worth asking the positive question: "What about a time you chose to trust God? What have you learned from these two experiences?"

- "What can we apply to our lives about the way God entered this world in human form? How could this change the way we live in our family context?"

J. O. Terry suggests these questions:

- "What would you have done if you were X?"

- "Is anyone in the story like you?

- "Has anything similar happened to you?"
- "If this story is true, then we should . . . ?"[2]

There's a huge range of possibilities. The more we try new ideas and evaluate them, the faster we'll improve in our question-asking skill. Listen to the questions others ask and use their ideas.

Questions that increase our sense of awe and mystery. Kevin Bradt, a Roman Catholic priest, points out that the Enlightenment brought about a desire for a sense of closure and completeness in life. As a result we started to fear mysteries. We wanted to solve them, understand them and control life.[3] But life does contain mysteries, and the Bible "does not answer every question."[4] Bradt suggests that "childlike awe, wonder . . . is the perfectly appropriate reply to Israel's stories of her wild, untamed God."[5] Interestingly, he also says that one of the most appropriate ways to share with modern people is to use stories: "It is precisely this . . . humility, circumspection, and intrinsic tentativeness toward the knowledge it conveys that recommends story as a model . . . to postmodernism."[6]

I've discovered this to be true in my own storying experience. It's enormously beneficial to relax and be content with areas of mystery in our faith—to not have to have the answers to every question. Often we get pushed into these areas of mystery by the kinds of questions listeners ask—for example, questions about why God gave us freedom when he knew we'd misuse it. A man of forty-five recently asked me in the local market why God chose to bless Abraham when he was a liar and basically sold his wife to save his own skin. (Note: I did not tell this story in my initial set of stories but in a follow-up set.) Good question! It led to a fantastic discussion of the Bible and then also why, of all the people in this town of fifty thousand, God allowed him to hear the stories.

Questions about the Trinity also reach this unanswerable point eventually. We can say something like, "This is a great mystery, but I've become content to realize that if I understood everything about God, then I'd be equal to him. I expect there to be areas that are beyond my comprehension. This is one of them, but each year I appreciate more that God is a Trinity."

These kinds of questions begin to proliferate the more stories people hear. When we get to the miracles in Jesus' ministry, we might ask, "Why did Jesus raise only three people from the dead during his three-year ministry? Surely more people than that died during that time. Only one of the three was a friend. If Jesus had the power to raise the dead, why didn't he use it more often?" This has led to many interesting discussions when I've asked it. It's particularly helpful because there's a danger when telling the miracle stories of giving a wrong impression—that is, that Jesus healed everybody and we can expect the same today. The reality is that he didn't, and it wasn't always easy to predict whom he would heal. Sometimes he healed people because they asked and sometimes when they didn't. The widow never asked for her son to be raised—she probably didn't think it was possible and may not even have known who Jesus was or noticed him passing by. Luke records that when Jesus saw the woman "his heart went out to her" (Lk 7:13).

Sadly, as in Paul's day (Gal 2:4; 1 Tim 1:3), there is much false teaching around. One popular modern teaching promises that if your faith is big enough, God will give you health, wealth and anything else you want. People are tricked into believing these promises because they sound so wonderful. In many cultures these beliefs also fit into people's previous religious ideas in which gods exist primarily to bless people. In contrast, Jesus promised that the gate and way would be narrow and the way difficult for all who followed him (Mt 7:14). Just before his death he warned the disciples that all believers would be persecuted (Jn:15:18-21). Struggling with why God works in these ways and doesn't do what we expect leads to a more balanced and biblical view of his purposes.

Questions that are partially unanswerable help people see that although the basics of the Bible are simple and clear, they're not simplistic. There is enough to keep the most brilliant mind occupied for an entire lifetime. Also, they help people maintain the balance necessary in a world that wants material blessings but doesn't want to follow the master who was persecuted and misunderstood.

Questions that generate pre-story discussion. This is something I have only just started experimenting with after reading about it in one of J. O. Terry's storying books.[7] He suggests that we start by asking people what's going on in their lives. This may give us a natural bridge to our story or indicate that today is not the day for our prepared story. For example, if there has been a huge grief in a person's life, then we'd be better off telling a story that speaks to this situation rather than something unrelated. Or if someone is struggling with family relationships, then address that area.

Lilly and her sixteen-year-old daughter were fighting constantly. This issue dominated Lilly's thoughts and prevented her from hearing stories on what she regarded as unrelated topics. Careful questioning revealed that the problem was more subtle than it at first appeared. Lilly worked as a beautician and her only child was plump. Lilly had started commenting on this several years earlier and made it plain that she viewed her daughter as unattractive. The result was not that her daughter started eating less and started a fitness program. Rather the problem became worse and her daughter started to rebel strongly, which included putting on even more weight. She did not feel accepted by her mother and gave up on receiving her mother's love and appreciation. Although we'd already reached the fourth story in our series, we decided to return to the creation story and discuss it with a stronger emphasis on the practical implications of being made in the image of God. For the first time, Lilly really engaged with the story. Lilly's daughter turned up at the next storying session and actively participated. It was obvious that God had begun to change Lilly's heart. She even complimented her daughter in different ways during the session.

Terry also suggests that we use pre-questions to set up a story and build anticipation for it. For example, before the Noah story we could ask, "How would you cope if you had to endure years of ridicule for doing something you thought was right?" Or perhaps even better, "Have you ever been laughed at for doing something you knew was right? How did it feel? Did you persevere?" This easily bridges to, "Today's story is about a man who experienced frequent ridicule. Let's hear why and what he did."

One helpful pre-story task is to get the listeners to retell the previous story before you tell the new one. This often starts discussion when people ask questions they've been thinking about since the previous time. Prediscussion could also involve giving the hearers a listening task. For example, "Listen for how often someone in the story obeys or disobeys God. What is the result?"

Asking questions ahead of time works best when you've been telling stories for more than a week. However, recently I was able to do this during my first encounter with Mr. Lee, a thirty-year-old man who owned a bicycle shop. I'd been building a friendship with the Lees for a year and had only had short gospel opportunities so far. This day was rainy, so I was walking rather than cycling. Mr. Lee commented on this, so I stopped to chat and he started asking questions about my lifestyle. He was shocked to discover that I hoped to live in this country for thirty to forty years but that at any time God might ask me to go elsewhere. He was surprised that I would trust God to lead me where he wanted, even when I didn't know where that was. I said that I knew a story of someone else who followed God when he didn't know where he was going. I asked if he'd heard the story of Abraham. He hadn't. I gave a quick introduction and then launched in. Our prediscussion ensured that he was listening intently. At the end he greatly surprised me in turn by saying, "You are a descendent of Abraham because you are carrying the blessing he was given to us in this town, at the ends of the earth!"

Two Well-Tested Sets of Questions

Both of these sets of questions have been used in many countries and contexts by a wide variety of people. The precise wording and even the order of the questions is something you can experiment with in your situation.

Set 1

1. What is your favorite part of this story? Why?

2. What questions do you have about this story?

3. What do you learn about people from this story?

4. What do you learn about God?

5. What will you take away from this story? Or, What in this story will change your life this week? Or, How will you apply something from this story this week?

A Wycliffe Bible Translators missionary from Australia suggests that the second discussion question above be phrased like this: "There are things in this story that some people don't like. What are they?" He advocates this approach rather than "What questions do you have?" for two reasons. First, it does not set up the storyteller as a "teacher" and source of all knowledge. Second, this phrasing allows other people in the group to feel comfortable leading the discussion. There's less pressure on the leader to have the right answers to people's questions. Finally, this question form may give group members the courage to raise their own doubts in a nonpersonal way.

One way to help foster discussion is to first encourage people to discuss each question in pairs. Then ask them to share their answers briefly with the group. The leader can model a brief answer so that talkative participants don't talk too long. Certain individuals or groups won't wait for discussion time but will start asking questions immediately. A useful technique is to keep turning the question back to the group or even the individual by saying something like, "Based on the stories you've heard so far, what do you think might be the answer to that question?"

Set 2

1. What truths do you see in this story?

2. Which truth speaks most to you? Or, Which truth most moves you?

3. How will you seek to apply this truth to your life this week?

4. Who else needs to hear this truth?

I really struggled to use this fourth question initially but am growing in confidence with it. When I ask it, a parent might reply, "I need to share this story with my children this week because it will encourage them." Or someone else might say, "I need to share this with my depressed neighbor. It will give her hope." The question is aimed to help people think about passing on the stories. Wouldn't it be wonderful if everyone passed on Bible stories even if they weren't yet following Jesus?

Consider writing these sets of questions sets on two cards, one set per card—or even nine cards, one question per card. You could have someone in the group choose a card (either without seeing it or reading it ahead of time) and then read that question to the group. Next time, someone else chooses a card and asks the question. This helps people learn to lead the group from an early stage. Remember, there's no need to hurry with an individual or group that wants to discuss in depth. There's nothing wrong with spending two or more sessions on a single story.

Amanda has been telling stories for six weeks to a group of two or three ladies and the same number of children. During week five she experimented with asking a person to read out a question and lead the discussion on that question. The ten-year-old girl volunteered first. She made a rule that the discussion leader didn't have to answer the question unless they wanted to. That ensured that there would be no shortage of people wanting to lead. After leading the first question, the girl passed the card to someone else. This method worked well from the first week, and all members of the group have taken turns. It increases their involvement and decreases any pressure on Amanda.

Reflection

1. What do you learn from this chapter about leading discussion?

2. Do you have any fears about leading discussion? How does this chapter help?

3. Are you comfortable with having areas of mystery in your faith? Why or why not? How might someone's life benefit if he or she were more willing to accept mystery?

4. When you tell stories, what questions do you want to try first with your listeners?

Discussion Dynamics
More Hints

Five older adults were meeting to listen to stories. None of them had any biblical background or showed any interest in Christianity at all. They simply enjoyed hearing the stories while hoping to avoid the God of the stories. During the first three weeks, the minute the story ended they started talking about the latest gossip. No matter what question I asked to get discussion started, it didn't work.

Some individuals and groups will test all your skills. You will discover that facilitating discussion is an art form, not following a recipe. On one end of the spectrum you'll find people who refuse discussion altogether. At the other end you'll find people who engage in discussion at a high level, asking "why" and "how" kinds of questions. And, of course, in between is everyone else. We need the Holy Spirit's discernment and the wisdom that comes from making many mistakes to know how best to interact with people, wherever they are on the spectrum. And sometimes he will direct us not to do any discussion at all.

Reasons Not to Do Any Discussion

Here are some types of issues that might prompt us to avoid discussion altogether.

Education issues. In many countries the working class have experienced a great sense of failure and shame within the education system. Anything that reminds them of this experience makes them uncomfortable. They can react negatively if it begins to feel like "school" or an interrogation. Age is also a factor. Many elderly people have received far less education than younger generations. In Taiwan, the current generation often goes to tertiary level. However, their parents sometimes only finished secondary school and many of their grandparents studied only at elementary school level. Elderly women in particular may have only had a few years of education.

In addition, many countries' education system consists of memorizing facts, not discussing. Cultural factors also come into play. It may be considered rude to question the teacher. If the teacher can't answer, he or she will "lose face," so students avoid questions altogether. If we dive in enthusiastically and start asking questions that start with "why" or "how" and that involve reflection and analysis (things many Westerners value and are encouraged to pursue in our education system), they'll run away, either mentally or physically. It will appear like they're rejecting the gospel when in fact they're running away from our insensitive approach.

However, we must also be careful not to make assumptions. Two of the best question askers I'm storying with at the moment have had a poor education. One man sells roasted sweet potatoes. The other is a woman who sells dried fruit in the local market. They are curious people and raise deep, thought-provoking questions. One day they asked questions that led to a long discussion on the Trinity.

Gender issues. In certain cultures there is little mixing between men and women. Listening to a story might be acceptable but they won't feel comfortable to linger and discuss it. Discussion is done in mono-gender groups.

Power issues. Certain countries have a clear class delineation or a concept of superior and inferior. People may feel uncomfortable having a discussion because they view the storyteller as either superior (and thus they are afraid to discuss) or inferior (and thus beneath their notice).

Personality issues. Some people just don't like discussing. They prefer to listen and go away to do their thinking. We need to be sensitive in our approach to discussion. We must not automatically assume that we understand why people seem uncomfortable. Sometimes it is worth gently probing and others times we just commit it to prayer and trust the Holy Spirit to work. His work is not limited to whether people are actively involved in discussion.

Trust issues. Sally works in two main contexts: a prison with women in their thirties and forties, and with middle-aged prostitutes. Few women in either group have completed secondary education. Sally struggles with the fact that the women don't ask questions or seem responsive. I wonder if this is due to trust issues. If they were to show interest they would risk exposing their hearts in front of the other women and also perhaps being reported to others.

Those who have lived under a repressive regime, been influenced by any religion that discourages questions, been hurt or are naturally distrustful may take time to trust the storyteller. Once they feel safe they'll often ask an initial question that isn't too important to them. If the storyteller answers sensitively, they'll increasingly ask their real questions. However, when the Holy Spirit is working, people usually become intensely curious. They'll start to ask questions and often start to read the Bible, despite not having picked up a book in years.

A mother and daughter I know are fish sellers, and they are currently hearing stories. I've told three stories and found that they become uncomfortable if I ask any questions other than, "What is your favorite part of the story?" I find myself feeling disappointed but remind myself that asking questions and discussing issues are not requirements for becoming a Christian. I can trust God to work.

Pushing an Advanced Individual or Group

One of my early fears with storying was that some people would be too sophisticated for it, whether because of their intelligence, learning style, length of time in the church or education. We can be tempted to avoid storying with these kinds of people and thus prevent them having a stimulating learning experience. The key is learning how to push the discussion to a higher level.

A short-term team from a theological college came to Taiwan to learn storying, and I wanted to give them a chance to hear a set of stories. I felt foolish as I started because I knew that this group knew their Bibles well and were exposed to the best teaching. However, I need not have worried. They were gripped by the familiar stories. We just pushed the discussion questions to higher levels and also encouraged everyone to ask their own questions about the stories. We had wonderful, lively discussion times and we all progressed in our understanding of our awesome God. Appendix A suggests some kinds of questions you can use with a group like this.

Answering People's Questions

Hopefully those with whom we are storying will start to ask lots of questions. Our temptation can be to answer these questions quickly and move on. It is also easy to fear questions—particularly those we won't know how to answer. Here are some principles.

If you don't know the answer, say so! It is terrible to watch people who are afraid not to know everything. They will make up answers rather than admitting they don't know. The truth is that we gain people's respect when we say, "I don't know." So simple, but what freedom to be released from the tyranny of having to know everything. If you're stumped, ask the listeners what they think. Their thinking might stimulate yours. Another approach is to say, "That's a great question. I'll go and think about it or ask someone else and see if we can find an answer." This answer validates the question, encourages listeners to keep asking and forces us to learn.

People are also encouraged by realizing that we're not all-knowing because it means they can start sharing stories with others without having every answer. They're more likely to want to start doing evangelism with others if they know they're free to say, "I don't know but I'll find out."

Be slow to answer. Often others have things to say in response to a difficult question. Recently I was storying with a couple and another man. They'd been hearing stories for six months. One of the men asked a difficult question about the Trinity, and the other man's wife answered beautifully, even though she was not yet a believer. About two months earlier, she'd asked me the same question. She not only remembered but had obviously thought it out for herself. If I had jumped in too quickly with an answer, we all would have missed out. Asking, "What do you others think?" will often result in all of us being encouraged by what the Holy Spirit has revealed to others.

Even if you're telling the story to only one person, be slow in answering. Ask your listener questions so she can work it out for herself. She will learn far more that way. Andrew and Jo's seeker group included a young Chinese migrant. After hearing the story of Jesus' death he asked, "What is the difference between someone who was a Christian their whole life and then dies and someone who does bad things their whole life and then trusts Jesus at the end?" Andrew restrained himself from answering and instead asked the young man what he thought based on the stories he'd heard. The Chinese man paused and then said, "The result will be the same. They will both go to paradise because it's all about trusting in Jesus, not what you do."

Don't answer beyond the stories told so far. If someone in your group asks a question that will be answered in a later story, just smile and say, "Great question. That will be answered in three stories' time." This keeps people curious and wanting to hear the whole story set. If we do delay answering a question to a later date, we must make sure we remember to do so. Our remembering communicates to our listeners that they and their questions matter.

Joy is ten and part of an adult storying group. In the middle of a discussion on Jesus' healing of a woman, she suddenly asked a question related to evil spirits—the woman's lameness is linked with them (Lk 13:11). Rather than answer the question that day I said, "Next week's story will specially talk about evil spirits. Can you wait a week?" She grew excited because she knew she'd asked a question the others hadn't and that her question would be the topic for a whole week's discussion.

What If Someone Totally Misunderstands a Story?

This happened to Dave while he was in Turkey. He told the story of the wedding banquet from Matthew 22:1-14. When asked what they learned about the king they replied, "The king was a bad man, because not even his guests wanted to come to his son's wedding. It was also wrong for the king to kick out the guy who didn't have wedding clothes. He should not have judged him for that." Dave was left speechless and unable to cope with this situation.

One of the reasons this might have happened was that this was the first story the listeners had heard. No Old Testament stories had been told before the group jumped straight to this parable. Interpreting parables is not an easy skill because listeners need to recognize that the main character is usually God. Knowing that allows us to import a lot of what we know of him from earlier stories. These listeners were interpreting the story in terms of the only reference they had—their own culture and experience.

When listeners give an answer that is off track, there are a number of ways to deal with it. The easiest is to ask the other group members what they think and whether they agree with the interpretation. This not only gives you a few seconds to pray hard, it often happens that someone else in the group has a different view. This person may be more spiritually perceptive than the first and so God graciously rescues the situation through a nonbeliever.

Another strategy is to ask clarifying questions. It might turn out that the person is not so far out as you initially thought. As he explains further, you might discover the "brick" in his thinking and say something helpful or use another story to come in from another angle. In Dave's situation, he might have asked, "Why do you think the king was bad? Could there be another explanation for why the people rejected his invitation?" Perhaps he could have explained about the wedding custom where everyone had to come in the correct door to receive the free gift of wedding clothes from the host. This was part of his welcome and grace to them. The man without the correct clothes had obviously not come in the correct way. Therefore the host had the right to ask him to leave. The man's failure to wear the correct clothes showed his contempt for the king's generosity. Eventually Dave could have made clear that the guests were expressing their contempt for the king, not because he was a bad king but because they didn't want to accept his kingship. They wanted to run their own lives.

Sometimes, however, we might simply have told the story badly, so we need to apologize and have another go. I did that recently and after the second telling my group had a fantastic discussion. Having a second try also gives your listeners more confidence that in the future they won't have to be perfect storytellers either.

If people are already reading the Bible, it's far easier to pull them back to the text and put things in context. If the disagreement is over something you've said, go back and read the biblical story. Through this process, pray for God to make his word clear. He has rescued me many times when I've been surprised by a weird interpretation from a listener.

When and Where to Add Illustrations

In the past I often added good illustrations into the body of the story. Now I prefer to keep the biblical story separate and use illustrations during discussion time. This not only honors the authority of Scripture but keeps the stories reproducible for others to learn. Here are a few illustrations you might find helpful.

Branch illustration. A coworker introduced me to this illustration. It can be used repeatedly throughout a set of stories because people's minds are rigidly fixed on the idea that children are born "innocent" and that our sin problem is less significant than the Bible tells us it is. The illustration works best if you bring two branches or twigs with you or snap them off a tree or plant in the course of the illustration. However, if you don't have a branch you can draw a tree and branch or even demonstrate using your arms.

"Originally people's relationship with God was like a tree and a branch. God was the tree and Adam and Eve were the branch. Their ability to live, grow and produce fruit was based entirely on God. However, they decided to rebel against God and be independent. The branch removed itself from the tree."

At this point I show the first branch that has been plucked off the main plant or, even better, actually break a branch off the plant right in front of them. "Does the branch look like it has any problems?"

"No, it's still green and healthy."

"But what's the problem with this branch?"

"It's separated from the roots."

"If we wait a few days what will happen? . . . You're exactly right. First it will wilt. Eventually it will be like this dry, dead branch." (Show them a dead branch. Try to select two branches from the same kind of tree or they'll get distracted from the main point.) "If I go and water this dead branch, will it grow again? Can it, of its own strength, go back to the main tree and reconnect itself? Nothing we can do no matter how hard we try, can ever give us new life. What is the only power that can give new life?"

"The Creator."

"What God promised Adam and Eve (although I doubt they understood it) was that one day God would provide someone who had the power to reconnect them to God. To restore the broken friendship and give new life. He was promising a Savior!"

Reuse this illustration at any point in the stories when someone tries to claim that we can earn our own salvation. Keep the dead twig nearby and pull it out and ask if they remember this illustration. Don't be afraid of repetition. The human heart clings to the illusion that we can save ourselves.

Freedom illustration. A common question listeners ask after the Genesis 3 story is why God gave Adam and Eve freedom if he knew they would misuse it to rebel against him. Ordinary family life is a rich mine of illustrations that are effective because nearly everyone can relate to them. Ask the listener to imagine two similar situations but to note the difference.

Situation one: a husband is somehow forced every morning at 8 a.m. to say to his wife, "I love you." Situation two: The husband has total freedom to say what he wants. One morning at 8 a.m. he says to his wife, "I love you."

Say to your listener, "The words and the time are the same. What is different?"

The person should say something like this: "The second time the words have meaning. His wife would be much more pleased by him saying the words by his own choice."

You then reply, "God did not want to create robots who would worship him and say, 'I love you' mindlessly. If we had no choice, any love or worship we offered would be meaningless. So God gave us the freedom to choose. This free choice infuses love and worship with meaning."

Sometimes I add, "We know that this freedom of choice was important to God because even though he knew we'd misuse it, he still chose to give it to us. This decision was going to cost him dearly. You'll find out more about that in later stories."

Clothing illustration. This illustration can be used after the crucifixion story. You say something like this: "When we are born we immediately start choosing to go our own way and not God's way. Each time we do this it's as if a bit more dirt gets on our clothing. As we get older our clothing becomes dirtier and dirtier. Even if we choose to rebel just once it's enough to make us too dirty to be in the presence of a perfect, holy God.

"When Jesus came he was perfect. So it's as if his clothing was what color? Yes, sparkling white. When Jesus died on the cross he was representing us. It's like all of our dirty clothing was piled on top of him and he was judged (given the death penalty) for our rebellion. However, because of who Jesus was—God himself—he had the power to deal with the 'dirty clothing'. His resurrection proved that Jesus had dealt with our rebellion problem.

"Now we are all faced with a choice. We can decide to wear our own clothing and one day we will be judged on the basis of that choice, or we can take off our dirty clothing and give it to Jesus. He is willing to give me his clothing in exchange. So now what color am I wearing? That's right, white. Does this mean I never go my own way again? No. Inside the clothing I am still an imperfect person, but now God accepts me because I'm wearing Jesus' perfection. You could even say, 'I am wearing Jesus'—hence the 'in Christ' vocabulary of the Bible. God relates to me and loves me because I am 'in Jesus'! I can go to heaven because of Jesus, not because of anything to do with me."

It's best to conclude by reading 2 Corinthians 5:21 and explaining it using the main points in this illustration. In a Chinese context I'm able to add a little more. The Chinese character for "righteousness" is made up of two parts. The character on the bottom is "me" or "I" and above it is the character for "lamb." I write the bottom part of the character on the paper and write the words for God above.

"When I rely on myself, God's anger remains on me because he must judge sin. He cannot be reconciled to me because of my rebellion. The perfect and imperfect can't mix. However, if I accept the death of Jesus the 'Lamb of God' (Jn 1:29) in my place, then the situation is changed. God looks down from above and sees Jesus and therefore declares me righteous. With the 'lamb over me' I am now able to relate to God. Not because I've become perfect but because of Jesus."

Become a collector of illustrations. If you hear a good one or think of one, note it. Practice it and polish it. If it doesn't work, just discard it.

Dangers to Avoid

Here are some common pitfalls of storytelling that will make your conversations less effective and meaningful.

Talking down to adults. This seems to be mainly a female tendency, especially for women who have taught Sunday school. Adults (children too, actually) hate to be talked to as though they were children. Most storytellers just need to be made aware they're doing it and then they can easily control it. Bible stories are for adults too and will challenge them too. However, if we use a voice for little kids, they'll be put off.

Adding morals. Bible stories are told in such a way that the teachings within them should be picked up by the listener. What people learn from a story is generally far deeper than a simplistic moral. In fact, it's encouraging when a listener picks up something we've never noticed or thought about. This often happens when we tell stories to people of different cultural backgrounds because they see things from different angles. Recently, a woman who views herself as unintelligent immediately observed something in a story that I had only noticed last year. She said perhaps Daniel didn't want to eat Nebuchadnezzar's rich food because he didn't want to owe a kind of debt to the king. He wanted to have the freedom to serve God without obligations. If I'd added a shallow moral to the story, I'd have missed hearing this woman's wonderful insight.

Becoming the authority. This is a great danger and one for which we must be alert from the first time we tell a story. The danger is even greater if we work with nonliterate people who cannot so easily "check up" on us. Often deep in our heart of hearts we like being the authority. It can feel good to have people asking us questions and thinking of us as knowledgeable.

To protect yourself against becoming the authority, differentiate early on the difference between your word and God's. Be careful to learn direct quotes as accurately as possible. When making a guess about someone's motives or thoughts, use words like, "possibly," "perhaps" and "likely." When training others to tell stories, explain this point to them carefully. For example, in the story of Noah, I might say, "Probably Noah's neighbors came and asked him what he was doing. I'm sure Noah would have told them that God was going to judge the world through a flood, and the only way they could be saved would be to get on this boat. . . . "

Also, never allow anyone to quote us as the authority. Jump on this immediately (but gently) and say something like, "I'd prefer if you didn't quote me as the authority. The important thing is what the Bible says. What does it say on this issue?" After a few reminders most people soon stop this habit. Encourage people as early as possible to start reading the Bible. Urge them to compare the story they've heard with the real thing and explain that we, as ordinary people, are not perfect and can get things wrong. They really need to look at God's Word for themselves. Everything must be compared to that. Also, ask them to let us know if they think our story was not faithful to the biblical text.

Introducing Bible Reading

Some people hesitate to use storying because they fear it will more easily result in heresy. This misunderstanding is based on the belief that storying prevents people from reading the Bible. Actually the reverse is true. Storying stimulates and encourages Bible reading. I constantly go back and check details. This is both because I suddenly feel compelled to check and also because I'm forced to do so. Some listeners will query details or even the way the story is told, asking, "Are you sure that's right?" Storying, done properly, actually decreases the likelihood of heresy because correction within a group is part of the process. In contrast, preachers, lecturers and other forms of Bible teachers are far less likely to be corrected. Most hearers wouldn't dare confront them because the context and style of teaching doesn't encourage it. So far I've found that there is far less heresy among the groups taught by storying than those within traditional teaching contexts. Storying is a more interactive process.

Although we want to encourage people to read the Bible, even in Western countries we can't assume that people will like reading or be willing to read. Sometimes other forms of media need to be used to "wean" them onto the Bible. In Taiwan, we prepared a series of mini-Bibles to ease people into reading the Bible for themselves. These mini-Bibles were prepared with the Bible Society using the modern version of the Chinese Bible, which is much easier for working class people to read. The first mini-Bible contains Genesis 1–4 and has an attractive painting on the cover. I give that to people after they've heard those stories. These mini-Bibles also have enlarged characters because the common complaint is that in most Bibles the characters are too small. We've just completed another mini-Bible with about five chapters of the Abraham story. We then have the Daniel story and various New Testament sections. Unfortunately, we don't yet have the Noah or exodus stories in mini-Bible format. I have photocopied the appropriate chapters for the Noah story and given them to interested people. If you do this, make sure you explain what all the numbers are in the text as they may be confusing to people who haven't read the Bible before.

I am also blessed with a very biblically accurate set of comic books that cover all the narrative of the Bible.[1] In Taiwan, there are lending libraries full of comics only, so it is a culturally appropriate form of communication. Unfortunately, in some comic books the art dominates the text. That is, the art really is more important than the text and so the stories aren't accurate or leave important sections out. We need to show discretion in what we hand out to people.

Many people appreciate listening to the Bible in a recorded format. Christian bookstores routinely stock some form of Bible on compact disc. Bob was a man who drove long distances for work. He found that listening to the Bible was an immense help and redeemed what could have been wasted time. Mrs. Chen didn't like reading and needed glasses, so she listened to the stories on a simple MP3 device. Inexpensive MP3 players can be powered by USB into the computer, batteries, or even solar and wind-up power.[2] The main question to ask is, "What will best help this individual get into God's Word for himself or herself?" The best method can be related to learning style, personality, lifestyle issues, cost and many other factors.

The more educated people are or the more "thirsty" they are to know the truth, the more likely it is that they will read the Bible for themselves. Most commonly I suggest Genesis 1 through Exodus 20 and Luke and Acts first. People with more interest will ask for more or just keep reading. Amanda was so hungry for God's Word that in six weeks she read from Genesis 1 all the way into Acts and then soon finished off the New Testament.

In Taiwan, many locals are functionally illiterate. Although they can read, they almost never do. Their learning comes via nonprint sources like television and radio and through life learning. It's exciting to see these people start reading because they suddenly want to read. Or those who are truly illiterate learning to read in order to read the Bible.

To keep the Bible as the focus of your storying, you might want to try this idea from storytellers in the Philippines. The storytellers explain at the beginning that they will tell stories from the Bible only. They physically draw a circle or explain that it's like they're standing in a circle. If people ask a question that requires their opinion or speculation, they step outside the circle. Thus they use a physical movement to differentiate between the story and anything that is added to the original story. This includes explanations of any religious jargon.

Remember the five adults from the beginning of this chapter who didn't want to do any discussion? After the third story they began to respond to the question, "What's your favorite part of the story?" They also started to ask occasional questions of their own. One of them has started to listen to the Bible on an audio player. Will this group one day discuss enthusiastically? I don't know. As the natural leader of the group starts to lead more, I suspect that he will have the skills to know how to help them to share. Whatever happens, I know they've begun to listen and apply things. The village leader regularly says things like, "God will save them or judge them." The grandma suddenly said after the exodus story, "If these stories are true and we tell them to others, then one day the doors of the temples in this town will be closed and no one will go to them!"

Action

1. Go through the stories you've chosen and start thinking of possible discussion questions for each. Include possible pre-story discussion or ways to help people note something in the story to come.

2. Do you know any illustrations that might help explain main points? Practice them until they are clear and fluent. Check with someone else for feedback.

Reflection

1. Can you think of any other dangers to avoid while storying?

2. How are you going to avoid falling into these dangers?

3. Take time to think through how to avoid becoming the authority. Why do we struggle with this one? What could be the results if we do become the authority?

PART FOUR

PASS IT ON: Training Others

The Basics

A team of fifteen workers in Central Asia requested twelve hours of storying training. Another group at a large church in Singapore only had two hours to become more effective sharing the good news with elderly people. Amanda, who as a brand-new Christian wanted to share with her friends, colleagues and family, started learning stories as part of one-to-one discipling. A group of university students wanted to learn how to use storying in the context of evangelistic Bible study groups. A missionary requested training over the Internet using Skype.

Each of these training opportunities had a different purpose and time allotment, ranging from two to twelve hours at a time to many hours week by week. The styles of training were also vastly different. Some were one-to-one and face-to-face and some were via the Internet. Some were small groups, some were individuals and one was a group of sixty-five Sunday school teachers as part of their bimonthly training. Many of you will train in your home culture, but others will train crossculturally using different languages. Your religious and social contexts will also be different. You may be training Sunday school teachers, university students or church lay people who want to reach their friends and family or disciple someone. Whatever your context there are basic principles that apply. This chapter aims to give you enough hints to make a start.

Work Out Your Purpose for Each Person or Group

Our purpose is always going to be strongly influenced by how long we have. An initial training period can range from ninety minutes to four hours. The shorter the time, obviously, the less that can be covered. It doesn't help anyone if we try to squeeze four hours of training into ninety minutes.

With story training, any session that's four hours or less is just an introduction. In four hours it's possible to offer a basic understanding of why storying is a wonderful tool and get started learning one or two stories. Hopefully this introductory time will lead the group to want more training. This happened recently with a group in a small village in Taiwan. The group had never had any evangelism training at all and couldn't really comprehend what evangelistic story training might be like. They initially invited us to do a ninety-minute session with the elders and deacons. It went well, and they subsequently requested more training and opened the training up to more people. We then did three sessions of ninety minutes and learned the two main stories from Genesis 1–3. A core group within that initial group then wanted to do more. So far, they've learned all the Old Testament stories, and several want to go on to the New Testament.

My current introductory training strategy is to meet three times spaced out about one or two weeks apart. The group or individual learns the first two stories (Genesis 1 and 3) and then we link these with the *Jesus* film, which serves as an introduction to the New Testament stories. This is only an initial training set. The week apart allows each person the time to tell the story to five to ten people. Ninety-minute to two-hour training sessions give people enough time for practice and discussion. Often people will ask for sixty-minute sessions, but results are better with a longer time. My hope is to find enthusiastic people who want to learn more stories and then arrange follow-up training.

Here are some questions to answer as you work out your purpose for a particular training session.

Are you planning to do more than just train storying? You may need to spend some time discussing questions such as, "Why share the gospel?" "What prevents us from sharing the gospel?" "What is the gospel?" We cannot assume people know these things, and the right motivation for sharing the gospel is key. If someone is motivated by guilt or the sense that "we ought to share with others," he or she is unlikely to engage in evangelism. Evangelism is an overflow from the heart. It's only when we get enthusiastic about the gospel ourselves that we will naturally share it. It's also crucial to discuss the issue of fear—the main hindrance that keeps us from opening our mouth.

Another one of the most important parts of training is sharing the enthusiasm we've acquired from using storying ourselves. If we sprinkle the training with real-life stories, this will help inspire people to try storying on their own. Once they begin telling stories to friends, ask them to share with the other trainees. The excitement of new learners frequently spurs on others in the group.

Whenever we are asked to train an individual or group, we need to think about what we know of the group: who they are and what kind of people they'll be sharing stories with, whether they've had any previous evangelism training and, if so, what was covered. Then we brainstorm what topics to cover. Next we start to arrange them in order and prepare from that outline, making sure the training follows a logical flow. Each topic is something like a single block or brick. You prepare the topic as a unit (be sure to note how long each topic takes to train) and then simply "connect" different topics together to suit a particular group. Once the initial hard work is done, all subsequent preparation is simple.

Are you going to train the whole set of stories in a short period of time? The Central Asian team training of twelve hours enabled me to share all the stories and train the group in all but three of them. We focused on the key stories and the most complex ones; we did not include Noah, Christmas and the resurrection because these are relatively easy to learn once you've learned the other stories.

We also trained the group how to prepare their own stories. Thus they received the tools to continue learning on their own. The disadvantage was that our conference site was removed from people we could practice with. It's ideal to go out each evening and share stories with real people.

Are you training one-to-one or in a group? Training normally proceeds faster in a one-to-one situation because the learner has your undivided attention. If the person is self-learner (unfortunately this is rare), you might be able to train the first few stories and then the trainee can listen to a recorded version or, even better, use the biblical texts go prepare his or her own story sets. Having trainees prepare their own stories is best, especially in situations where the local culture is different from the trainer's context. The bigger the group, the more time you'll need. Once a group is more than twenty participants, it's harder to train. So try to gain experience with smaller groups.

The Basics of a Training Session

One approach to training in storying is to use five basic hand motions to accompany five steps. (Obviously, if these gestures are inappropriate in your culture or don't communicate what they're supposed to, change them or get rid of them altogether. They're just a tool.)

1. Listen: Hands cupped behind ears. The trainer first tells the story straight through so that everyone has a chance to hear it. Some learners will need to be told, "Please don't open your Bible or write notes; just listen." Many of us are so used to taking notes that it's almost reflexive to open our notebooks and start writing. But the idea here is to "see" the story—like a movie in our minds— not to follow a set of written reminder notes.

If you're working in your own culture with literate people, it's okay for the group to learn your story. But make it clear that this is just a basic pattern. You'll keep improving your story, and so should the trainees. Your personality and context influence how you tell the story, and the same thing will be true of the trainees. The goal is for everyone to end up sounding like the unique individuals they are, not to end up sounding just like their trainer!

Keep in mind that literate people have often crippled their memories by relying on written notes to remind them of things. Sometimes they need extra help to learn stories. A cartoon strip may be helpful as a memory prompt (more on this below), but if it proves a hindrance, don't use it.

If you're training crossculturally, it's far more important for trainees to work out stories themselves. Give them a Bible passage and guide them through the process of preparing a story. Encourage them to use idioms and speech patterns their culture will appreciate—that is, encourage them to speak naturally. One way to offer encouragement is to praise the people who are already doing this. Let them share their prepared stories with the group. This lets the group know that they shouldn't sound like the trainer. Keep stressing that the biblical text is the pattern. They must not change its emphases and must remain true to its meaning. Once the trainees have prepared their stories, get several volunteers to tell them. Let the participants comment on the strengths of each story.

Training longer stories such as that of Abraham or the exodus is more challenging. Try prereading the passages out loud or listening to recordings of these chapters. Then have the group decide which story sections are essential, and read or play those sections over and over again until individuals can tell the story. You can also prepare a series of shorter stories and then link them. For example, my Abraham story includes Genesis 12:1-3, the initial call and the promises God makes to Abraham. Then I include the "failure" story of Genesis 16, where Abraham doesn't trust God to give Sarah a son. Then I focus on the restating of the promise in Genesis 17:16-22 and 18:10-14, where both Abraham and Sarah laugh at God. Then there is the birth and naming of Isaac from Genesis 21:1-7 and Abraham finally trusting God completely in Genesis 22. My story concludes like this:

Abraham lived until he was 175 years old. Before he died he saw the first promise fulfilled—that is, he'd had sons and seen their children. However, the second promise (that his descendants would have their own land) wasn't yet fulfilled. God explained that Abraham's descendants would have to wait four hundred years for that because the sin of the people in Canaan wasn't complete yet. Abraham was content to trust God that this promise would be fulfilled. When Abraham died, the final promise was partially fulfilled. His family had been richly blessed, but this blessing hadn't yet reached the whole world. The subsequent stories will tell you how the world was blessed through the descendants of Abraham. That blessing can come to you living right here in [name of city or country].

My cartoon for this story has five squares. In squares one, three and five there is a picture of a present or gift to represent the promises. The first promise is of descendants—it's difficult to become a great nation without them. Promise two is that Abraham's descendants would have their own land. The final promise is that "I will bless you and through you all the nations of the earth will be blessed." Square two is an "X" for failure to trust God, and square four has a checkmark to represent success— Abraham trusted God. Obviously this is a literate person's cartoon, as all the symbols are abstract.

ABRAHAM

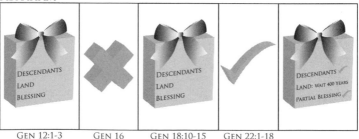

GEN 12:1-3   GEN 16   GEN 18:10-15   GEN 22:1-18

If those you're training cannot read, here are two methods you can use. (You can probably think of others. It might even be helpful to ask the group how they'd prefer to learn.) My first suggestion is to have a reader read the appropriate passages out loud (or use Bible recordings) and then get members of the group to retell the story. An older woman in one of my recent trainings told a brilliant story after hearing the biblical text once. Storying can allow illiterate people to shine in front of their literate church members.

My second suggestion is to have a person from your group's culture prepare and tell the story, then have the trainees practice telling the story with someone who can read checking that they don't deviate from the text. The closer the storyteller is to the trainees in terms of culture, the better this method should work. If someone like a missionary tells the story and trains that story, it may not be organized in the way that stories are told in that culture.

If there are no Scriptures in the local language, Bible stories will be the only way people can hear the gospel. There will be a need to develop many story sets.[1] In the past, Bible translators tended to translate the whole New Testament first. Thankfully translators and evangelists are beginning to cooperate more closely, which means that Genesis and Exodus 1–20, other essential parts of the salvation narrative, and Luke and Acts are being translated before other parts of the Bible.

2. Tell: Hand opening and closing in front of mouth (almost like a beak). In this step, the listeners immediately practice the story they've just heard, first in groups and then in pairs. If a group particularly lacks confidence, they can group-tell the story twice or even more times. If you do this, have people tell different bits of the story than they did the first time.

If the storytellers want to tell the story eventually in a language other than the one being used for the training, they are welcome to launch right into that. During a seminar at the Third Lausanne Congress in Cape Town, South Africa, I trained in English, but people immediately told stories in a variety of languages—French,

Swahili, Chinese and many others. There was quite a babble going on, but it made it easier for trainees. It also communicated that storying is for every people group in every tongue.

After trainees have heard a story several times and told it, there are ways to learn it more fully. The story can be turned into drama or song. Volunteers can tell the story to the group. The more repetitions the better. And the more a person struggles with confidence, the more he or she will have to practice. This is particularly the case with working-class or village people. They may have been told all their lives that they're "stupid" and, sadly, they often believe it. So they may need lots of biblical encouragement and reminding that God loves to use the weak and will be with them to help them tell the story.

3. Discuss: Two hands in front (like two beaks) facing each other and "talking." During training, discussion takes two forms. The first is what you'd actually do with hearers—that is, discuss the actual content of the story. The second is a discussion focused on trainees' questions about sharing the story with others. They may want to know why you've chosen certain stories or told them in a certain way. They need to understand how you decide what kind of discussion to initiate with hearers. Then they'll feel free to experiment on their own.

Keep emphasizing that we don't know all the answers. They need to keep praying that the Holy Spirit will guide them and take them on their own adventure of discovery. Whether I'm training church members, new Christians or Bible college graduates, I'm amazed by how much more there is still to learn from these basic stories. Adjust the level of the questions and they will suit any group of hearers. But even if a group is highly educated, don't neglect the simple questions: these sometimes trigger the deepest discussions.

4. Application: Hand placed on heart. The application step can be initiated by a discussion of straightforward application-oriented questions or in less traditional ways—through drama, poetry, song, art, puppetry or dance, for example. A nontraditional approach was modeled to me during a missionary conference with at least seventy attendees in which we studied Elijah's life from 1 Kings 17–19.[2] Each person was asked to choose whether they wanted to be in a drama, poetry, song, art or dance group. The groups were then given about twenty-five minutes to prepare the story or part of the story in one of these forms. Each evening the groups would present what they'd prepared. We were skeptical that we could produce poems and songs in such a short time. But we did. Our poetry group particularly struggled at first to learn how to work together since writing poetry is normally a solitary activity. Here is the majority of a poem on 1 Kings 18 that our group of about six people wrote:

Victory

Ahab arrived in regal robe,
Elijah rough and scrubby strode.
"You troubler of Israel," Ahab said.
"Not me; God says it's you instead."
Elijah challenged the evil king.
Why hadn't Ahab thought of this thing?
"Excellent! Bring the prophets out,
We'll see whose power can end this drought."

Two sides opposed on a mountaintop,
Four fifty, eight fifty against one foolish flop.
Each sacrifice awaiting fire,
Which god's breath would most inspire?
Heathen priests with raucous cries,
Slashing wildly as all hope dies. . . .

The man of God stacks up twelve stones,
Water carriers serve with groans.
Soon sacrifice, wood and stones are drenched,
And water even overflows the trench.

Alone but calm Elijah prayed words few,
"Prove you are God, bring all the people back to you."
Fire flashed from heaven in one great blast,
Incineration and evaporation happened fast.
False prophets by the hundreds died,
The One True God was glorified!

Each evening we not only laughed but heard the stories over and over until they were deep in our hearts and minds. Eighteen months later I still find myself thinking about Elijah and how these stories apply to me. The short preparation time was intentional. It's been found that the longer people are given to prepare, the more they'll strive for a perfect presentation rather than concentrating on the biblical content. These presentations can be used in a meeting situation to encourage the group or form part of an evangelistic presentation on the street or in other contexts.

In cultures that value the performing arts, this might be the best way to do storytelling. Miriam Adeney has included various suggestions in her book on Muslim women.[3] She suggests pairing gifted storytellers and composers so that each story people learn has an accompanying song. You could sponsor workshops to develop culturally specific songs or dramas, maybe combining biographical songs or dramas with thematic ones. There is unlimited potential to develop tools that help people not only remember the stories themselves but go out and share them with others.

Adeney reports that a song-and-dance troupe in India developed forty-eight songs, accompanied by drama and dance in their traditional style, to tell stories from Abraham to Nehemiah. They gave five-hour performances (perfectly normal there) night after night. Imagine the impact of that. All because whoever trained them gave them the freedom to use their God-given gifts to come up with creative and culturally appropriate ideas.

Similarly, a group in China held a two-day training. The leaders trained five stories from the creation to Abraham. After each story they had groups develop a song, poem, dance, rap, drama, picture or anything else they wanted to represent the story. On the final night they held a performance to present all they'd done. The audience loved it. And all of the material can be used to share the gospel in rural villages.

This combination of story, song and movement deepens the impact of the stories in our hearts and minds and makes them almost impossible to forget. It allows all learning styles—those who learn by doing (kinesthetic learners) as well as those who prefer hearing (aural learners) or seeing (visual learners)—to benefit. Our role as trainers is to trust the Holy Spirit and allow him to set our trainees free to honor God in culturally and individually appropriate ways. We need to be humble enough to rejoice when our students become better storytellers than we are. Then we can fade into the background and let the Holy Spirit do his work.

5. Share: Two hands held together, palms up, move in arcs to the right and left toward "the ends of the earth." Decide on appropriate homework for each story. Experience suggests that the stories need to be shared with five to ten people each week to be remembered properly. Obviously this is a bit unrealistic in a conference situation—two times each night might be more appropriate. Even better, ask the group what they think is reasonable. Each participant could set his or her own goals.

Practical Tips for Group Training

Here are some things to keep in mind when you're working with a group of individuals learning stories.

Room size. Training in storying involves moving around and practicing stories, perhaps with song, dance and drama components as well. The practical implications are that you need a good-sized room and perhaps side rooms for these activities. If the room is too small, the noise will become so great that those who can't work with noise or distractions will struggle to learn.

Seating. A casual setup works best. Consider starting with chairs in a semicircle or even an oval with the facilitator seated at one end. The chairs need to be easily moveable so that participants can form first small groups and then pairs. Certain cultures may never use chairs at all. In Central Asia, we all sat on carpets. Training can happen anywhere: under a tree, on a boat or in a car.

Numbers attending. Limiting group numbers helps ensure better training. Twenty is about right. The less experience you've had training, the more you need to consider limiting the numbers. If participants have undergone a selection process, they might be more keen to learn.

Training a large group. The Sunday school teachers in a Singaporean church held training sessions every two months. I was asked to train them in storying for elementary-age children for two hours. Sixty-five teachers showed up, and space was cramped. So each participant prepared a story individually, which included reading the story and then practicing out loud. The trainees could only murmur their stories out loud because of the space restrictions. They also spent time imagining themselves in the scene. Then they broke into pairs and shared the stories. Later, we were able to split them into poetry, song and drama groups by using stairwells and one extra room. Sometimes creativity is necessary to make the best use of space.

A friend of mine uses what he calls "peer training" for large groups. First, he shares the basic principles for preparing stories with the whole group. Participants then work in pairs to prepare stories, often with each pair taking a different section of a longer story set. The pairs practice the stories with each other and critique each other. At the end, each pair tells their story in order. My friend reports that "people get excited as they see it all come together in order."[4]

Storying in general returns to the basics of human communication without fancy gimmicks. Sometimes technology is a help, but usually storying benefits most from simple presentation methods. Whiteboards, large sheets of paper, and paper on which to sketch cartoons are all useful tools. Of course, if you're working with illiterate learners, avoid making them uncomfortable with the trappings of the literate world.

Megan attended a twelve-hour training session in Central Asia. She'd arranged to stay in a village with Muslim friends afterward, and having just learned the stories she thought she'd try at least one. The family group was tri-generational. Megan felt that her local language ability was limited but had heard that storying made this less of an obstacle. The listeners loved the first story and told her to keep going. Over the weekend she told stories up to the Passover, and they didn't want her to leave. "Come back soon and tell us more stories," they begged. Megan soon passed on what she'd learned to other expatriates and locals.

James participated in a two-hour seminar and learned stories from Genesis 1–3. Though his learning was basic, he immediately realized the potential of storying. The first listeners who heard his stories were a group of international students. After James finished his stories, he looked at his watch and was horrified to discover that he'd talked for an hour. He apologized profusely, thinking he'd gone on far too long. The students said, "Keep going; don't stop! When we attended those courses explaining Christianity and the New Testament, we didn't really understand them. But this we understand."

James became a missionary in a creative access nation—one where traditional missionaries aren't welcomed. He used storying widely in one-to-one evangelism and in group situations. He often invited other missionaries to listen in. They were astonished and told him, "We've never seen such discussion and response from nonbelievers with any method we've used." That motivated those missionaries to start storying too.

When James went home to Australia he tried storying in his home church, which was hours from the nearest big city. His first attempt was with thirty people; two-thirds of the group were young people and the rest late-middle-aged. He wasn't sure whether the two groups would mix. All responded positively, saying that this was the first time they'd seen everyone involved and contributing in any church gathering.

Reflection

1. When the time comes for you to train others, work through the sections in this chapter and develop a training for your particular context. Appendix C contains a training checklist.

2. Who could you train?

3. What kinds of poetry, drama, dance and so on are prominent in your culture? How could these forms be used for God's glory?

MOTIVATING TRAINEES

Since Amanda had become a Christian after hearing an initial set of stories, it would seem natural for her to want to share those same stories with others. However, this wasn't the case. Although she personally loved the stories, she wasn't convinced that others would listen. In fact, she perceived me as the "professional" and preferred to bring others to hear me tell stories. I was unwilling to do this as I wanted to equip her to share effectively. Local people are the ones who will continue to live and work in this part of Taiwan. So unless the locals start storying, the impact on the area will always be limited by my available time. If I didn't train anybody and then moved away or stopped storying for any reason, that would be the end of people being able to hear the gospel through this method.

Amanda had many issues to deal with. Primarily she felt fear: fear that others would laugh at her storytelling efforts, fear that she would be rejected by family and friends and become isolated, fear that she couldn't learn the stories. She compared herself negatively to others. She felt she didn't have time and wasn't mature enough. Any or all of these reasons could easily have prevented her from even trying storying. I tried many strategies to help her become a storyteller. Some worked and some didn't. Each person is different and will be motivated in different ways.

Like leadership, evangelism and teaching, storytelling is best "caught" rather than "taught." In any effort that involves learning and growing, people need to be motivated to get over their initial fears and resistance to new things. Talking about storying seldom motivates anyone to want to try it. For most of us, we need to actually hear a demonstration story to grasp the idea of it and see the implications for how to use it in our lives.[1]

After various frustrations in trying to motivate Amanda and other learners, I read David McClelland's research on social motivations.[2] He found that although people experience many motivations, most can be grouped under just three main areas: the need to achieve, the need to belong and the need to influence. I was primarily using the motivators that affect me: the need to influence and the need to achieve. I suspect that many Westerners are motivated by these two. However, non-Westerners are more motivated by the need to belong. I wonder if they struggle to use many evangelism methods because they often involve stepping out individually from peer, work and family groups to be different. They set up potential conflict. But evangelism in groups (gathering for meetings and working together to hand out tracts) is appreciably easier. I am beginning to learn how to use the "belonging" motivator in training.

Following are the methods I've tried, which generally fit under the three motivation categories, although some may fit in two categories.

The Need to Influence

To inspire others to want to use storying, I often start by sharing my journey. Amanda, like many others, heard me telling stories and assumed that I was born with this ability. I've had to remind her many times that the first story I told was far from perfect and in fact was rather boring. Amanda did a better job with her first stories and I told her so. Many cultures are much better at telling stories than we are. She needed encouragement to keep going because she had perfectionist tendencies and was tempted to give up.

I also scatter numerous stories of people's responses throughout any training. These stories are all about how real people have responded to the stories. Share how you initiate conversations and what kinds of people you've shared with. Also, talk about the kinds of questions listeners have asked and what touched them as they listened. Even stories of our failures can be useful if we've evaluated them and learned what we did wrong. The things we've learned can prevent others from making the same mistakes. People love to hear these stories and to know that the trainer isn't just talking about theory. I've met some trainers who don't use storying themselves in evangelism and discipleship. This tends to destroy their credibility. Using someone else's stories doesn't have the same impact as our own.

Try to choose stories that suit the listeners at that particular training. That is, in a Western context tell stories of Westerners' responses, and in a Muslim country share about storying with Muslims. Also, ask new trainees to report back about their experiences. It's easy for trainees to dismiss my stories by saying, "Oh, she's just good at this method. She's had years of experience." It's harder to dismiss someone who learned the story the same day they did and is already enthusiastic about it.

In 2005 I led a fifteen-hour training time in Central Asia. Fifty people came to the five afternoons of training. My hope for the week was that everyone would learn the first story and tell it to at least one other person. From the third day on there was time for people to share their first storying experiences. One local lady, Jemillah, owned a small shop that had continual electrical problems. During the training week, Jamshed had to come out again to fix her electricity. As he finished Jemillah said to him, "I want to thank you for your hard work on my shop. You are always patient and come quickly. For a long time I've been trying to think how to thank you. I would like to thank you by telling you a story that brings life and hope. It has changed my life and I hope it will change yours too." She then told the Genesis 1–3 stories. Jamshed asked her whether on following visits she'd tell him more about the Savior who was to come.

Another way to inspire people is to take them with us. Nothing beats hearing the stories being told in a real situation. It's even better if the learner also tells a story. Recently an OMF apprentice came to visit me for a few days. Her purpose was to start learning the stories so she could use them in her situation. I trained Amy on the first three stories. First she watched me in action. Then I asked two sisters who sell pork if they'd be willing for Amy to share a story she'd just learned. They were willing, and the nervous storyteller told the story of Noah while standing behind their main business counter. She did an excellent job and the ladies enjoyed the story too. Afterward Amy and I immediately discussed what she'd learned and prayed that God's Word would burrow deeply into these ladies' hearts. That simple experience fired Amy up more than any amount of training.

The Need to Belong

The first way to motivate people through belonging is to match them up with a prayer partner for encouragement. Find someone who will pray with the learner about getting out and telling stories. This includes praying for opportunities, for courage and for the particular people the trainee wants to story with or with whom he or she has already shared. This mutual encouragement can help a trainee feel part of a team. The more sets of prayer partners there are praying for each other, the more participants will feel part of a community working together to share Jesus with others. Prayer partners can also hold each other accountable—an achievement motivator—and share inspiring stories—an influence motivator.

I have recently started stressing that storying increases a sense of community and can improve family relationships. That is, it can result in more family and friends coming to Christ and thus builds a community of believers. Amanda has noticed her friendships deepening through storying even before people become believers. Not only does listening to stories draw them into a community, but relationships deepen as people share their lives, values and thoughts.

Here is something I tried with a group that was really struggling with the fear of ridicule and rejection. The fear of "breaking up" community was severely inhibiting this Asian group. So I drew up this chart. As people arrived for that evening's training, they marked how many people they'd practiced with and the listener's responses.

Number of nonbelievers shared with	Number of Christians shared with	Negative responses	Neutral or indifferent responses	Positive responses

I was hoping that positive and neutral responses would be the majority and negative responses a minority. This has been my experience, and so it proved that day. There was only one negative response, and further inquiry revealed that the participant had set herself up for rejection. She shared with her younger sister, with whom she often fought. She also admitted that her tone of voice made her sound superior.

Members of the group were surprised at how many positive responses there were from their Buddhist and Taoist family and friends. This simple chart showed them that what they'd most feared—ridicule and rejection from their friends—wasn't what happened in reality. In all my storytelling I've had only two really negative responses. Are we going to let Satan make us fearful on such a low probability?

Neutral responses, where the listener doesn't respond enthusiastically or start asking numerous questions, are common. Responses are often neutral in contexts where people don't ask questions until they've learned to trust you. A neutral response may also be a personality thing. People who are shy, lacking in confidence or not naturally curious simply ask few questions. Sometimes a lack of questions reveals that the listener is not yet spiritually open. Hopefully as the person hears more stories he or she will become curious. Sometimes it is worth telling just the first two stories and letting the listener know you'd love to tell more stories if he or she is interested. That is, use the first two stories as a kind of filtering system to find seekers. I pray that people will become spiritually hungry and I await God's timing to continue the series.

Fearful people often first need to gain confidence in an less threatening, more easily controlled context. They might start by sharing with other believers. Natalie is shy and finds the idea of sharing stories with unbelievers difficult. I've suggested that she tell a story after every church service to someone she feels comfortable with. Hopefully she'll find people who want to hear the whole set. I've also encouraged her to share with people on the outskirts of the church. These people might be nonbelievers or undiscipled believers. At the very least sharing stories with these people gives Natalie practice and builds her confidence. However, it may also disciple or bring someone to salvation. Sometimes listeners such as these want to begin learning stories themselves and so push a new storyteller into training them.

Another way to support learners who need extra assistance is to set up story opportunities for them. John was especially reluctant to tell stories, believing that men wouldn't listen to them. I took him to a contact of mine and said, "I've been training John to tell stories. He's a bit nervous about sharing them. Would you be kind enough to let him tell you a story?" A request like that is hard to refuse. I stayed for the story and helped with the discussion afterward. Then we debriefed and prayed for the couple who heard the two stories. Sometimes we might need to accompany people like John a second time or even more often.

The Need to Achieve

Many people have a need to achieve, and if they are going to share the gospel they want to do it well and see a positive response.

However, sometimes these perfectionistic tendencies prevent people from even trying storying. This was the case when I started training in storying. The underlying reason was that my earlier stories were too complicated, including too many questions and too much commentary on the Bible story. Thus people who weren't like me couldn't learn the stories and gave up after only a few attempts. The solution was to simplify the stories.

Learners motivated by achievement often start with stories that are too complex. They tend to add too many details into a story they're trying to prepare or attempt too much at once and need to break the task into smaller pieces. Try to work out ways to help them simplify their story.

Richard, a missionary to northern Thailand, was introduced to storying at one of my seminars. He liked the concept but found that he struggled to learn the stories and so didn't use the method. Richard was different from me, so my style didn't suit him, and I didn't know enough at that point to train him more appropriately. Eventually Richard went to a Simply the Story seminar, where he learned simpler methods to learn and tell stories.[3] He also had it reiterated that he wasn't meant to memorize the story. Once he simplified the learning process, Richard found he was free to tell stories as part of his normal life. During the course of one day he told a new story to his wife, a few stories to his English class, a story to his Thai golf partner and other stories to his children.

In another case, I was helping my Bible study learn to tell stories. Over a two-year period we discussed the stories, they learned all of the set, and finally they were encouraged to use the stories. But they didn't. Some made a few attempts, but it wasn't becoming a natural part of their lives. The problem was that I'd underestimated the amount of practice people need before they're confident sharing stories. We are now going through the whole set for at least the fourth time. This time members of the group spend one week practicing a story or two with each other, and the next week we go out and tell stories. Each one of the pair must tell a story to someone. Whether because of personality, learning style or confidence level, some people simply need more practice.

Debriefing, that is, reviewing how the storytelling went and evaluating how it could be improved next time, is particularly useful for achievers. It allows us to learn much more from an experience than we would without it. For example, if people in a group aren't sharing stories, we can gently ask what is preventing them. Then we deal with the obstacles within the group, giving group members the opportunity to offer practical suggestions. Whether someone's experience is positive, negative or neutral we can ask, "What did you learn?" Often we learn more from failures, mistakes and negative experiences than we learn from success and positive experiences.

One day a fish seller in the market told me she still didn't understand the stories I was telling her. I was astonished; I'd thought they were simple enough. Now I'm asking myself what the reason is for this. Are the stories too difficult? Is it that my Taiwanese isn't clear or simply that she believes she won't understand me and so doesn't? (This sounds strange but is fairly common when certain people are faced with a foreigner speaking their language.) It is possible this woman can hear the story and understand the words but is struggling to see its relevance to her life? I don't know the answers. Her daughter standing next to her has no problems, so I've asked the daughter to retell the story immediately to her mother. Hopefully they'll both absorb it better.

Debriefing after negative experiences and failures can help us learn that we need more practice or to pray more. After a positive experience it can help us realize how amazingly God assists us and gives us the words we need. It is helpful to start each training session by having members of the group share their experiences and then spend some time debriefing with them.

Evangelism can be a frustrating experience for achievers because it is not just a matter of "I share and they come to new life." We need to deal with misconceptions about evangelism, but we can also help by creating smaller goals for them to meet. Achievers often benefit from concrete goals, such as, "Share five stories this week." Or they might keep a list in a notebook of the people they've shared with and their responses. Even if no one repents and believes on the spot, they've still achieved their goals.

Steve and Shannon of Illinois were in Romania conducting a vacation Bible school (VBS) in a village of about 3500 people. The adults in the village were deeply suspicious of the VBS team and would not have listened to stories from them. But the missionaries taught the Romanian children stories from Genesis 1–4. The songs, games and crafts supported the story of the day. To the missionaries' surprise, the children hadn't heard any of the stories before. Each child was given a journal and asked to tell the stories to adults, who would sign the page as evidence they'd heard the story. They didn't tell the children how many times to tell the story and were astonished that not only did every child tell a story but that one boy of about twelve told seventy-two stories! At the end of the training, the final tally was more than nine hundred stories told over four days.

Later Steve and Shannon used the idea of a signature card back home in the U.S. On the back of the card was a "letter to the listener" that explained the purpose of the storytelling and the child's assignment. They included the reference for the story because they'd found that many people would read the story for themselves to check the details. They'd think, "That's not in the Bible," and then find out that it was. Although the enthusiasm using this method wasn't as great as in Romania, most children told at least one story during the week, and many unchurched people heard stories. To encourage achievers in similar situations, you could award certificates for trainees who learn a certain number of stories. Or award people who tell a certain number of stories.

The main thing is to bathe the whole process in prayer: before, during and after training. I once had a group with which I tried every possible method for motivation. But they still struggled to get over their fear and lack of confidence. As part of the training we talked and practiced ways to deal with fear. In the end I was left with the best method of them all—prayer. Their hesitancy reminded me that the most important motivation comes from the Holy Spirit. Sometimes it just takes time for God to work. I can be too impatient.

Problems Often Encountered

A persistent block lingers in some trainees' minds that stories are for children. Or they fear that adults won't listen and so they practice only with children. When giving homework I allow people to tell stories to children but they don't "count" in terms of practice times. This is not because children aren't important but to encourage people to story with adults. We want to see parents becoming Christians and raising their children in a Christian home. Parents are encouraged to tell stories to their own children as this builds up the family and disciples the children.

It can also be a challenge to know when to start training a new believer in storytelling. This will be different for every person, but try to start as early as possible. If someone has heard us tell one story and then learns it, the size of the task seems manageable. If he or she has heard us tell fourteen stories, it can seem overwhelming. We need to remind this person that we've practiced each story many times. The key thing is to give people confidence that the Holy Spirit will help them tell stories. Encourage their efforts and help them prepare good stories.

Also, be sure to pray for them. This is a spiritual battle, and Satan will do his best to discourage them and make them fearful and discouraged. He fears storytellers (as he fears pray-ers, disciplers and evangelists) because he knows how effective this method is.

What about training nonbelievers? This is something I have just started to experiment with. A friend of mine recently suggested that after telling a story we ask, "Who else needs to hear this story? Is there anyone among your family and friends who would benefit from hearing it?" Then we go home and pray that the stories will be passed on. The next week we can very casually whether anyone told the story to someone else. After each subsequent story we ask, "Who needs to hear this story?" Let's see what God does. At the time of the exodus and the exile, it was often nonbelievers who were passing on the stories. Otherwise how did Rahab hear the stories of God's miracles in rescuing his people from Egypt? She heard enough to risk her whole life and trust God (Josh 2:9-13). Later on, the kings of Babylon and Persia passed on news about God's deeds—for example, Nebuchadnezzar (Dan 1–4), Cyrus (Ezra) and Darius (Dan 6).

Recently I told five stories to a group of five adults. Then I was scheduled to go overseas and miss a week. The natural leader of the group said, "I'll retell all the stories while you're gone to help the older ones review." This is the kind of response I dream about. More common in my experience is people telling others that they should listen to the stories but not actually telling them themselves. Bronwyn had this experience. She was a language student, searching for a simple method to share the gospel that was less limited by her language ability. Ah-May, a middle-aged lady in the market, was patient with Bronwyn's language efforts. Over a hotpot lunch one day Bronwyn shared with her the story of creation. The woman seemed to understand, but Bronwyn wasn't sure the story had made any impact. Five days later Bronwyn revisited her market stall. Ah-May took her to the lady next door. She animatedly insisted that her neighbor listen to this story.

Ah-May was a little afraid of her friend because she spoke to spirits and had dreams that foretold the future. But although Ah-May had heard only one story herself, she seemed to sense a truth in it that her friend needed to hear. This began a weekly pattern of sharing a story: creation, the fall, the flood, Abraham and the Passover. The women's eagerness for the stories outstripped Bronwyn's language ability. Whenever Bronwyn was ready with a new story, they were ready to hear. Gaps and breaks did not seem to matter.

Unbelievers who drag others along to listen to gospel stories are exciting. Even better would be unbelievers who naturally pass on the stories to others. Up to this point, I have seldom trained unbelievers to tell the stories. This has been due mostly to my lack of faith, since I doubted that listeners would want to pass them on. Now I'm starting to teach listeners the stories immediately. I emphasize that it will help them remember the story better. Then I casually suggest that they share the stories with others.

What about Amanda? I'd tried many of the motivational methods above. She needed far more practice than I'd realized and then suggestions of how to find someone to story with. Her relationships at work weren't at a stage where she could ask people to listen. But she could tell stories as she walked in the cool of the evening. She could ask a friend to accompany her and conversation would flow naturally.

I kept asking Amanda whom she might story with and tried to help her to see her contacts in a new way. Eventually she said she had two friends who ran a cosmetics business who wanted to hear stories. We arranged for an initial time to meet. Amanda still wanted me to tell the stories and said, "You'll do a better job; they'll prefer to hear you." I refused and explained that her friends hadn't heard me tell stories and so couldn't compare. Amanda would learn far more by having to trust God and share herself.

From the first week Amanda did an excellent job. She's thrilled that God is working through her. The women come with their children, ages ten and thirteen. These children have been an asset because they ask challenging questions and make perceptive comments. We also started training these listeners to tell the stories from week one. Last week it happened. The children again led the way by telling the creation story to their grandfather. We hope for more. And Amanda is gaining confidence and telling stories to other people in a range of contexts.

Continual Improvement
The first time I tried telling a Bible story I sounded stilted and boring.

God has since brought about dramatic improvements. If communicating the good news is important (which it is), then we will strive to keep improving in our communication of God's Word. Even after telling the stories hundreds of times, we'll hone and polish them. We'll keep checking the details against the Bible. We'll keep working on the exact words to use and think carefully about what nuance each communicates. We'll work on the rhythm of delivery and our tone of voice—and we'll see improvements every week.

One way to improve is through self-evaluation. Whether this is a useful tool depends somewhat on our personality. Some people are too perfectionistic and end up getting negative and depressed. Others are too easy on themselves. A happy medium might be to ask ourselves, "Where were the weaknesses in this story? How could it be improved?"

We can also ask others to evaluate us, either formally or informally. The informal approach is simply to tell a story to friends and ask them what they liked and what needs to be improved. Then keep practicing until it feels right and is compelling to listen to. A more formal method is to arrange a group coaching session.[4] One person in the group gets up to tell a story. Before beginning he or she says which of three levels applies. The levels are:

- Level 1: The storyteller tells the story with no feedback given (very few choose this level).

- Level 2: The storyteller tells the story and the evaluators say only what they liked about the story.

- Level 3: The storyteller tells the story and the evaluators say what they liked and what can be improved.

The rule is that the person being evaluated cannot defend himself or herself. Generally the group members will argue among themselves because they won't necessarily agree on the strengths and weaknesses. In the process, the storyteller can pick up a lot of useful hints. Next, another person in the group tells a story and the process is repeated. Not only do people being evaluated get to learn from the feedback to their own story but also from all the other stories.

James, who works in a creative access country (one where gospel work is politically sensitive) both telling stories and training others, says people love doing peer critiques—it's easier to accept criticism from a peer than from a trainer. James suggests peers evaluate one another according to three criteria.

- Clarity: Is the story in colloquial language without Christian jargon? Are there too many confusing names and details?

- Accuracy: Is the story true to the Bible? Has the storyteller added to, changed or interpreted the story? Has he or she left out something important or guessed at something? (For example, some versions of the Cain and Abel story make unfounded guesses about why God didn't accept Cain's sacrifice.)

- Naturalness and interest: Is the story overdramatized or told with an unnatural voice? Is it engaging?

So how much practice is enough? Most people aren't comfortable with a story until they've told it at least ten times. A story needs to be told twenty times before it's not easily forgotten. Storytelling is a case of "use it or lose it." Eventually you will have told the story often enough that you won't ever forget it.

The good news with Bible storying is that not only does it help you grow as a Christian but your storying ability can improve dramatically over a relatively short period of time. The aim of training others is to have them no longer need us and to "pass it on" by training still others. Note the motivational methods that John Walsh used, either explicitly or implicitly, in this situation.[5]

John was given the opportunity to do storytelling training in prisons in the southern United States. The course was four two-day-long sessions over a nine-month period. John was up front with the participants: "This is a nine-month training. Each time we'll give you homework. If you don't do the homework, you can't come back to the training. No exceptions. When we're done, we will graduate those who have successfully completed all the homework."

The inmates were taught twenty stories and had to use each at least five times. They were taught how to use the stories in daily conversation, on the prison yard, while waiting in long lines, in the cell blocks, in their churches and in group Bible studies. They told these stories to their friends, roommates and their husbands or wives when they visited. The most exciting thing for them was to tell these stories to their children. Many said, "My children don't listen to me anymore. They're ashamed of me. But they'll sit and listen intently when I tell them one of these Bible stories."

One chaplain told John, "I've never seen Bible studies go so deep before. This method takes the inmate to new levels of Bible study and discussion." An inmate pastor from a state penitentiary said, "I finally understand what you've been trying to teach us. I am preaching to my congregation using analytical reasoning, but the men in my church think in stories. I'm not talking in their language."

John started with inmates who were already believers and dedicated to ministry. Eventually, he allowed anyone to take the training. He saw nonbelievers get involved, learn the skills and eventually come to Christ. One woman said to him, "I was so tired of Christians talking to me about 'accepting Christ.' I simply didn't understand what they were talking about. It very clear to me now that I've learned these stories."

One of the graduates was sent to another prison during a river flood evacuation. He was put in the section of the prison that housed inmates with mental problems. One day he was out in the yard on a hot day. The Lord said to him, "Go sit at that picnic table."

He said, "Lord, I'm not wearing my hat. My head will burn."

"Go sit at that table."

So he took his Bible and went and sat in the sun at the picnic table. As he was reading his Bible, an inmate walked up and said, "What are you reading?"

"My Bible."

"Read it to me."

The storytelling graduate said, "What if I tell you a story out of this book?"

The man agreed, so he told a Bible story, and then another one. Several other inmates joined them at the table.

Every day, he went to the table and a crowd of men stood around as he told them story after story. Fortunately he had learned more than fifty Bible stories at that point. He said, "I was amazed how those mental patients stood out in the hot sun every day and listened quietly to the stories. But I was even more amazed by the intelligent questions they asked." This went on until the storyteller was transferred back to his own prison.

John concludes, "After nine months, my work is done. The instructors are now living in the prison."

Reflection

1. Can you think of any other ways to motivate people to want to tell stories, especially those who are motivated by belonging?

2. Which ideas motivate you most? What about someone you'd like to train in storytelling? If you don't know, try asking the person what he or she finds motivating.

3. Draft a training program for the person or group you thought of in question 2 above and start asking God to open the door for you to be involved. Perhaps start with training someone that you are discipling.

4. What would help you improve your storytelling? Is there a friend with whom you can practice?

5. Do a formal coaching session with another storyteller or in a bigger group.

PART FIVE

ADAPTING FOR
SPECIFIC CONTEXTS

Evangelistic Storying with Different Audiences

So far our focus has been on using storying for evangelism. However, storying has a plethora of applications. This chapter discusses different evangelism contexts, and the next focuses on various teaching contexts with Christians. In reality these situations are often mixed. That is, Christians and not-yet-Christians will often be present in any Bible study group, church service, university or youth group. Each section aims to give pointers the reader can develop further.

Basic Principles
Let's first consider the principles of adapting a basic set of stories to different contexts.

Principle 1: Prayer is always essential. As always, the preparation stage must be bathed in prayer. We can never pray too much. We ask God for wisdom about what stories to share, how to adapt them, how to lead discussion. We pray for God to prepare our listeners' hearts and that he would be glorified in how we share. We ask for wisdom in knowing our listeners and that we would be able to communicate truth to them. We plead that "prisoners will be set free" (Is 61:1) and "the blind made to see" (Jn 11; 2 Cor 4:4).

Principle 2: Know your listeners. This principle seems obvious but is often overlooked. The need to adapt our stories for our listeners is one reason the stories can't be memorized. A one-size-fits-all approach doesn't work. This is one advantage storytelling has over books. A book is written for a more generalized audience. Storytelling is for a particular audience or person. It is tailor-made.

The better you know a person or group the easier it is to choose the stories you want to share. It also helps you tell the stories. For example, in telling the exodus story in Taiwan I often mention that the Egyptians were like the Taiwanese; they "worshiped everything." The Chinese phrase doesn't literally have to mean "everything" but means a huge range of gods. These few words help my listeners identify with the story. They're not essential but increase the sense of application to their lives.

Knowing your listeners also helps with discussion. We're able to ask questions specific to the person or group rather than following a set "recipe." There are huge differences in the kind of discussion we'd do with a Sunday school class for eight-year-olds and what we'd do for a university group. Or for a group learning English and people in a nursing home.

Principle 3: Know your purpose. Our purpose will have implications for which story we choose, how long we speak and how we tell the story. Are we trying to simply introduce our listeners to the Bible and its stories and make them intrigued to know more? Or are we talking with someone who's really interested and wants to hear the whole set in a short period of time because there won't be another chance to meet up? Perhaps we're telling a story in a secular public speaking context, where we don't let on where it comes from but hope someone will come and ask. This latter scenario was the case with my friend Jeff.

Jeff was doing his final talk for a public speaking course. It was near Easter. He introduced his presentation like this: "In 2010

Easter Sunday was April fourth. In 2011 it was April twenty-fourth, and next year it will be April eighth. Sometimes it's in March. This change of date makes it hard to remember and hard to plan for without looking at a calendar. Why can't they make it easier for the working man and standardize the date? Why does it keep changing?"

Jeff then bridged into the fact that Easter is linked with the Jewish festival of Passover. "More than three thousand years ago the people of Israel were slaves in the land of Egypt. They cried out to their God to save them and to remember that he had promised to bless them. God prepared Moses and told him to go to Pharaoh and say, 'Let my people go.'" Then Jeff told the story of a Passover a little over two thousand years ago and the Passover Lamb who died.

Principle 4: Know the length of time available. A ten-minute session in a church service or playgroup is very different from an English class of thirty minutes. You might have a one-off opportunity of several hours on a bus or plane. Length of time dictates how long the story is, how many stories you can tell and how much discussion is possible. However, it doesn't always follow that if you have two hours on a bus that you'll be able to speak for two hours. The listener might only have the capacity or interest level to absorb one story. It's best to gauge someone's interest with a short story and then, if he or she is interested, continue.

Principle 5: Really listen! This principle is directed at myself. It is too easy to listen to others impatiently and mentally be preparing what we want to say next. This is usually obvious to the other person and communicates strongly that we don't care. We must learn to listen and respect the other person, even if we disagree with him or her. As we listen we'll also pick up hints for how to start sharing or how best to share.

Let's now consider how we might adapt storying for specific groups and situations, beginning with those from different religious backgrounds. I have chosen to consider only three religious groups to illustrate the thought processes needed to make adaptations. First, think about the brick-wall diagram for your particular audience, whether it be one person or a group. What are the "bricks" in their thinking? What beliefs do they have about God, the Bible, Christians and Jesus? The bricks will be different for every single listener. Even if someone claims a certain religion, he or she doesn't necessarily believe everything the religion officially endorses. And although we can share with someone of any religious background without knowing a great deal about their beliefs, the more we know, the more effectively we will communicate.

Storying with Muslims

Many who try using the stories with Muslims quickly encounter a major frustration.[1] The listener will keep saying, "You're telling the story all wrong. It wasn't like that." The Qur'an and Islamic tradition contain many Bible stories but in fragments and with significant details altered. For example, in the Abraham story many believe it was Ishmael who was to be sacrificed, not Isaac. Another version says Abraham's knife turned into a feather so that Ishmael wasn't harmed. How does a storyteller deal with these responses, which are not only frustrating but undermine our credibility as messengers and, more seriously, the credibility of God's Word?

First of all, these frustrations should remind us that evangelism is a spiritual battle. We are too prone to thinking that if we just explain clearly enough, people will believe. We need to remind ourselves that people are dead in their sin (Eph 2:1) and we cannot raise the dead. We need this reminder over and over because we forget it easily. Remember too that although Jesus was the perfect evangelist it didn't guarantee results. Also, every religious group has its challenges and blind spots. In Taiwan it is the blindness that asserts, "All religions are the same. They all encourage us to do good works." In a secular European context it is apathy, attacks on your source of authority and a tendency to ridicule all Christian belief as unscientific myth. We should not be surprised that evangelism is frustrating. Satan wants us to give up. We have a low tolerance for frustration and fear, so these are two effective techniques he uses against us.

Here are some responses that might help in the Muslim context. When you use them, be careful not to let your frustration show in anger. Keep a wondering and gentle tone of voice as you say something like, "It's interesting that your version of the story is different. I wonder why that is. When was your story written down?"

The Qur'an was written after A.D. 500, but it's best if the listener volunteers that information. You could even plot it on a line so there is a visual reminder. In the case of the sacrifice of Abraham story, the changes are dated even later than the Qur'an. The Qur'an doesn't mention the name of the son to be sacrificed. His identity as Ishmael is based on even later tradition.

Then ask (gently), "Do you know when the story I tell was recorded?" They probably won't. It was written down by Moses before 1200 B.C. Rather than telling your listeners the answers, it's more powerful to let them think for themselves. "So how many years earlier is the story I'm telling?" It might be worth discussing secular history and whether an earlier story (closer to the events) or a version more than a thousand years later is more accurate. The goal is to start raising doubts in their mind. If you make the point too strongly, you'll only make enemies and offend unnecessarily. Truth is often more effective stated gently.

Another strategy is to first allow your listeners to tell their version of the story. Model listening without interrupting, no matter how angry or frustrated you might feel. Then request permission to tell your version without interruption. Discuss it as normal but perhaps also discuss the changed elements and gently ask (perhaps rhetorically) why their version is so different.

It's also important to keep in mind that in Islam, the circumcision of males is tremendously important. Male workers in Muslim countries are often asked, "When were you circumcised?"

To be uncircumcised is to be unholy. With anyone other than Muslims or Jews, you probably don't need to tell the circumcision story in basic stories about Abraham. However, with these two religious groups you can later link it to the prophets, who say things like, "Your bodies are circumcised but your hearts are far from God. Circumcise your hearts" (Jer 4:4 is one version of this). You could finish the Old Testament stories by asking, "How can a heart be circumcised? The stories that follow will tell you how."

Sharing with Those Who Claim the Bible as Their Authority

Depending on their background, those in these churches might be as familiar with the Bible as the storyteller, or they may have never read it.[2] It will be obvious soon after you begin storying what the listener's level of Bible knowledge is. That will give you pointers about which stories to tell, how much detail to go into and the level of discussion questions to use. Some storytellers in the Philippines went to an area where animism was mixed with biblical content. The locals had generally never read the Bible for themselves and were dependent on their priests for their beliefs. But the priests only rarely taught the Bible and many revered or even worshiped Mary. The storytellers were viewed with deep suspicion by both the locals and their clergy. They clearly stated that they would tell only Bible stories and they soon won over their listeners. Over time, many locals compared their original beliefs with the Bible and came to new life.

For those who have an elevated view of Mary, one possible adaptation is to expand the birth story of Jesus. Either in the discussion section or for "homework" for more independent learners, suggest that they look up all the passages about Mary and write down what the Bible says about her. For less self-directed learners, you might look up the relevant passages and read them aloud and then discuss. Hopefully this will allow these listeners to see which of their beliefs about Mary are not scriptural. She was not eternally a virgin, as her other children are listed by name (Matthew 13:55), nor was she born sinless. What they might find surprising is how seldom she is mentioned and how humbly. She always points to the centrality and mission of Jesus.

With anyone who claims the Bible as their authority, keep saying, "Let's see what the Bible says." Continually take your listeners back to it and allow them to see for themselves which beliefs aren't biblical. Doing it this way is less confrontational and thus more effective.

Storying with Members of New Religious Movements

There are some major challenges with these groups.[3] The first is having an opportunity to share at all. Members of new religious movements often visit in pairs and tend to launch in with a prepared speech. Even if you have an effective conversation, you might not have another opportunity to tell stories because they'll report you to their leadership and be asked to avoid your house in future.

But may we never give up on anyone. All can be saved by the gospel as we once were. If you encounter people in these groups and want to try storying, remember to offer hospitality, as some groups believe they're the only hospitable people around. Provide snacks and drinks, but avoid caffeine. Allow them to share first, and really listen to what they say. Then request the same length of time to share. Major on the seriousness of sin using the branch illustration and Genesis 3, and perhaps ask them how to solve the problem of spiritual death and being cut off from God. Let them commit themselves to explaining their way of salvation. Then talk about the total impossibility of raising ourselves to spiritual life. Don't be afraid to drag this out a little. Then discuss the exodus story (a spiritual parable of salvation), the Day of Atonement (how God asked to be worshiped and how he dealt with the sin problem), and Jesus, especially his sinless perfection and his death and resurrection, pulling in Passover and the torn curtain symbolism from earlier stories.

Then you could give each listener a gift of Scripture and a tract explaining about someone who left that particular group and why. This means being prepared ahead of time. Having the literature wrapped as a gift is helpful. With new religious movements, an experienced person is usually paired with a less-experienced person. If one of the pair is more spiritually open, the other will prevent him or her from asking questions and visiting you again. Giving separate gifts might just mean that they get read. Surely it is worth the effort and expense. When I encounter members of new religious groups, I find myself praying fervently the whole time. These are times of strong spiritual attack and I find my thoughts saying over and over, "Don't waste your time. They'll never listen." I ignore these thoughts and remind myself instead what the Scriptures say.

Storying in English Classes

These are exciting days worldwide. People of all nations are moving around the world and coming into contact with the gospel. As they migrate, they are often more open to new ideas for the first year or two as they struggle to adapt and learn new languages. Churches have been at the forefront of classes for migrants. Many people have come to Christ through the sharing of the gospel and the care and hospitality that they've received from Christian groups at a lonely and bewildering time.

Using the stories in an ESL (English as a second language) context will obviously be affected by your participants' language abilities and the length of time you have available. One helpful strategy for your class preparation time is to make a vocabulary list of any unfamiliar words you're planning to use. During the class, you'll first spend time learning and using the vocabulary so that when your group hears these words in the story, they're already familiar with them. Here are some more ideas.

• Break the longer stories into shorter sections.

• Use simple questions.

- Encourage listeners to ask questions.

- Give them the biblical passages afterward in English and their own language so they can review on their own.

- At the end of a set of stories, give each person a copy of the *Jesus* film in their own language. Or point them to the online version.

- Give them a Bible or Bible portions in their own languages and show them where to read. (Just handing a Bible to people generally scares them. We need to put in a bookmark and show them how to get started. Also, we need to explain what the chapter and verse numbers are and how to look up a passage by using its "address.")

- Use more acting and pictures.

My home church in Australia has run an ESL program for many years. There is a Bible discussion each week, but at Christmas and Easter the church always invites a special speaker. When I'm home they often ask me to come and share because most of the students are mainland Chinese. I tell the stories appropriate to the festival and switch back and forth section by section from English to Chinese. Then we all have an international meal together with everyone bringing a plate of food. During the casual meal, students often come and ask questions. The church follows up by having Scriptures and *Jesus* films available in all the languages of their students.

Storying in One-Off Opportunities

When you use storying, ideally you'll have multiple opportunities to tell stories to a person. But this isn't always possible. Can storying be usefully adapted to one-off opportunities? Yes, as the stories that follow demonstrate.

But first, some basics. One-off opportunities are heavily influenced by the amount of time that's available and how many stories a person can cope with at a time. If I have only thirty minutes, I use the general pattern illustrated in the stories below. I'm learning to ask God for opportunities every time I travel on buses, trains and planes. The more I ask, the more I expect opportunities and the more my eyes actually see the opportunity when it's there in front of me. I seldom have the chance to share if I don't talk to my seatmate within the first few seconds of sitting down. Just a friendly greeting will do. This prepares the way for subsequent conversation.

In April 2010 I had a three-hour layover in the Hong Kong airport. A Vietnamese man sat next to me and soon we were in conversation. He turned out to have only thirty minutes before his flight. Our only common language was English, and I needed to simplify my English and speak slowly. He had never heard any Bible stories. He did think he had one Christian friend, but when he described this man's beliefs to me, it was obvious his friend was a Muslim. I only had time to share the first two stories and answer a few questions. In the last few minutes I told him how to find out more and where to go looking for Christians and Bibles. Out of the thousands of people in the Hong Kong airport that day, this was the person God arranged for me to meet. God can be trusted to multiply that brief opportunity and to arrange follow-up.

On another trip, I boarded a bus in New Zealand. There was only one free seat available, next to a young guy. I groaned inwardly. After four years in Taiwan I was sure I'd have little in common with this young man. However, I quickly reprimanded myself for this pre-judgment. I'd been praying for two days that God would give me a good gospel opportunity while I was on my holiday and that it would be obvious that he'd prepared the way. In faith, I opened my mouth and greeted him. He replied and we quickly moved on to general questions about who he was and what he did. He was nineteen and had joined the army as that was the fastest and most cost-effective way to get his truck license. Then he planned to resign and join his father's trucking business. With every word he said, I was thinking, "We have nothing in common! This can't be who God has for me to talk to." Suddenly he asked me, "What do you do?"

To answer this question simply by saying "I'm a missionary" is the wrong thing to do in the Australia-New Zealand context. The word is regarded negatively and often generates a hostile response, largely because of the media's portrayal of anything to do with Christians. So I normally give people a clue or two ("I live and work in Taiwan and speak Chinese") and let them try to guess. He was unable to guess even when I gave him follow-up clues like, "I have the pleasure of seeing lives totally transformed," or, "I teach the world's bestselling book—this book is really sixty-six smaller books and was written over at least one thousand years."

However, when I said, "I tell Bible stories and answer questions people have about life," he looked at me strangely. He said, "Two nights ago I had a dream and woke up knowing that I had to read the Bible but didn't know where to start!"

I needed no more hints from God! We only had thirty minutes, but there was just time to tell the Genesis 1–3 stories and then use a six-picture outline to summarize the rest.[4] I explained how the Bible works (two testaments, chapters, verses and so on) and wrote down my suggestions for him to get started reading it. We then only had time to say goodbye before we both went joyfully on our way. His parting words were, "God sent you to me today."

Sometimes a one-off opportunity might be long enough to share the whole set of stories, assuming the person can handle that volume. Once on a bus in Taiwan I had to sit next to a young man in his twenties who was doing his two-year compulsory military service. After I found out about him, he in turn asked about me. I said I was a storyteller and offered to tell him a story. He had never heard the creation story and was obviously interested to hear more. After the second story he was still interested. In three hours we covered the whole set and he still had time for a sleep between the Old and New Testament stories! I'm sure he was still thinking as he dozed. In order to complete the whole set and help him cope with the sheer amount of story, I simplified some parts and chopped out small sections.

Rob and Donna were working in an area after a major earth-quake. The people group was totally unreached. At Easter Robert was asked to share with a group of adults. One gentleman knew about Christianity and could read, but no one else had that ability. So Robert prepared a whiteboard and drew six or eight pictures that told the story of the Bible from creation to resurrection and beyond. The people were mesmerized as they followed the story. When Robert came to the part where Jesus rose from the grave, the people immediately responded by clapping as though they were cheering for their team.

Storying When Opportunity Is Limited

Sometimes our opportunities to share are limited by geographical distance. Neil and his elder sister, Jane, had experienced a pushy church where they'd been pressured beyond their level of in-terest. They'd begun investigating Christianity because of their sister's transformed life, but the material for seekers didn't suit them and they dropped out altogether. The Christian sister was upset about this and asked for advice. I'd only been doing sto-rying for about a year at that point but felt that this was what they needed. I'd never met Neil or Jane. They worked in their parents' restaurant. Our time was limited both by their strange working hours and the fact that I lived two and a half hours away from them. But both agreed to an initial meeting and requested to talk to me separately so that no other family members would hear the discussion. It took a little while for them to trust me but at the first meeting I told them the Genesis 1–3 stories and en-couraged them to ask questions. .

In the end we met four times and covered the whole basic story set. We spread out the meetings so that Neil and Jane could read the Bible for themselves in between. After the first meeting we all met together because they'd learned there was nothing to fear. Within a relatively short time both were baptized. They've gone on to be effective wit-nesses within their networks. I would like to have time now to train them. But again it would have to take place within the limitations of their circumstances.

I had another opportunity with the husband of a believer who didn't become spiritually open until after I'd moved away from the area. When I visited for a weekend, I set it up as a time for him to ask any questions he had. Over eighteen months I had about four opportunities during visits to share the complete story set and discuss his myriad questions. He has recently been baptized and is sharing with others. The advantage of storying in this kind of situation is that it provides boundaries. Both sides know approximately how long a session will take. After the first meeting, it is easy to set up the next time. Longer chunks of stories are told at a time, but they are linked with independent investigation and Bible reading.

Telephone and the Internet help overcome some of the challenges of geographical distance. We can direct people to a storying website or YouTube where they listen to the stories, then afterward we discuss them over the phone or by email. Technology provides new opportunities that didn't exist before.

Another limited opportunity involves telling stories to young children and hoping the parents who attend will be reached. Julie works in a highly multicultural part of Australia. Her church runs a play group once a week for young children. There are supervised play times, along with a craft, a snack, music and a story. Each child must come with a parent or grandparent, and these are key opportunities to talk to adults as the program is fairly relaxed. Julie decided to experiment with telling a Bible story. However, time was limited because of the young age of the children. Julie shortened the stories and was astounded at the interest of the six adults. Two were from a Muslim background. One said, "I love to hear the stories because I want to know what will happen next."

Storying with University Students

Harold, an engineering doctoral student in the United States, decided to try storying with a small group of his classmates. This wasn't an easy group to work with. It included skeptical agnostic mainland Chinese men and a Hindu woman from India. But every other week the group gathered faithfully to hear a story and then engage in a Bible study on one of the passages or a related passage. This approach worked well. Harold covered long sections of story at a time—for example, in the second week he told the stories of Cain and Abel, Noah, and Abraham. They studied Genesis 12:1-3 and Genesis 22, where Abraham is asked to sacrifice Isaac.

Harold was surprised at how quickly the group seemed to understand and engage with the material. The Hindu woman often took an active role in explaining things to the men in the group and was moved at times to tears by what she was learning. By the seventh week one of the group commented, "These are not just a bunch of simple stories. If you think hard, you will see that there are many connections between them." During the eighth week Harold led a time of questions and answers to try to clear up any continuing misunderstandings. This particularly helped clarify why Jesus had to die and what it meant to follow him. The Hindu woman even asked, "How do you become a Christian?"

Although none of the group became Christians at that time, Harold was amazed at how God drew them all closer to himself. He says, "I think they might grasp the gospel better than some who have been going to church meetings all their lives."

The main adaptations with this kind of group are with the discussion questions—how you ask them and at what level. Aim for more questions that start with "how" and "why." Encourage people to go looking in the Bible for the answers. One thing to be careful of is allowing Christians to dominate the discussion. Storying using the five basic questions from set 1 (p. 113) relieves this situation. However, occasionally you might need to privately ask Christians to say less or even to leave the group.

Storying with Men

Much of our evangelism is not masculine enough. Men don't generally want to be told that they're loved and accepted; they want to follow a hero on a grand adventure.[5] They want their lives to have purpose and significance. Understanding a few simple principles can radically change the stories we choose, the language we use, the themes we emphasize and the discussion questions we ask.

If two stories are appropriate and only one has a male hero, choose that one. For example, choose a healing miracle about a man rather than the woman bent over for eighteen years (Lk 13:10-17). Emphasize strong action and heroes. In discussion, challenge them to have courage to walk the harder road against the majority and why this is worthwhile. Ideally, of course, men should tell stories to men. In the beginning of the church planting situation I'm in, that has not been possible because there are no male coworkers. However, when I'm in a mixed group, I will aim my story at the man, not his wife or daughter. Women are seldom put off by stories told for men, but the opposite isn't true.

One adaptation I make to the Abraham story with men is to use the local term for "mistress" in talking about Abraham and Sarah's failure to trust God and the resulting relationship with Hagar. The term here is "little auntie," and I always say it in Taiwanese even if I'm telling the story in Mandarin because it communicates better. I say something like, "Abraham's wife suggested he take a 'little auntie' and Abraham didn't disagree!"

In the birth of Jesus story we can ask the men to tell how they'd feel if their fiancée became pregnant and they knew the baby wasn't theirs. It is a strong emotion they feel safe to share and it gets them involved with the story.

One of my follow-up sets of stories is a series on Daniel. I used to emphasize how he brought glory to God during his transition to a new context. However, I now bring those themes out in a slightly different way by focusing on the tremendous courage Daniel and his friends needed in order to take a stand among peers, coworkers and bosses. We discuss why they were able to be so courageous. Answers have included, "Because they knew that God was real. If I knew that, then he would be worth dying for."

Last month a story group was reflecting back to the Daniel stories where God repeatedly stepped in and miraculously saved Daniel and his friends. We were now talking about Stephen (Acts 6–7). God didn't save him and he faced a painful death by stoning. These hearers are still not following Jesus but they need to be prepared for persecution and see that following Jesus involves picking up your cross, not perpetual blessing like many portray Christianity. One man in the group was asked, "How could Stephen face that death with courage and die so well?"

The man replied, "He had seen Jesus and knew that Jesus had gone through worse suffering. He knew that Jesus was with him in the midst of this pain and that he would soon be eternally safe in heaven."

Reflection

1. Which of the basic principles of adapting stories to different contexts do you struggle with most?

2. What are some strategies that would help you improve your evangelism?

3. What applies to your context from this chapter? What have you learned? What other suggestions do you have?

4. How could you adjust your stories to be more appealing in a context that's different from yours? Consider groups of men, migrants, university students and different religious backgrounds.

5. Choose a specific cultural context for evangelism and come up with suggestions on how to adapt storying for that context.

STORYING FOR CHRISTIAN TEACHING

When it comes to Christian teaching, whether in a discipleship, small group Bible study, ministry training or theological education setting, the focus has traditionally been on studying the Bible by utilizing abstract teaching methods. Can storying be adapted for use in these contexts? Absolutely!

Storying in Discipleship

Even if someone is already a Christian, there are many advantages to using storying. For newer Christians it will lay an excellent foundation for their biblical understanding. After storying, any study of prophets, wisdom literature and epistles will make more sense. Storying has a major side effect: it contributes to biblical literacy. People become excited about the Bible and start to read it more. This might seem counterintuitive—after all, people could say, "I know the story so I don't need to read it." But experience shows that most people who hear stories want to read the biblical text themselves.

Many discipleship materials are topical studies (on anger, forgiveness and so on) or studies of the Bible's commands. Storying allows a different approach. Which makes you want to forgive more: the command "Forgive your enemy," or the stories of Stephen, Jesus and Joseph, who did exactly that? "Don't commit adultery" or the story of David and Bathsheba and its sad results? Stories and testimonies—both positive and negative—are powerful teaching tools.

Another key advantage of using storying for discipleship is in the area of rebuking and correcting, which 2 Timothy 3:16 reminds us is a key part of teaching Scripture. Westerners in particular tend to confront error very directly. Storying allows us to provide correction and rebuke in a way that's easier to accept. This happens naturally during a course of stories, but it might also happen that an issue comes up with a believer and we use a story to confront it in a less direct way.

This is exactly what Nathan the prophet did with King David. God sent Nathan to confront David with his sin of adultery and murder. This was a dangerous assignment. Nathan could easily have lost his life if he tackled it in the wrong way. But God gave him the wisdom to start with a story:

> "There were two men in a certain town, one rich and the other poor. The rich man had a very large number of sheep and cattle, but the poor man had nothing except one little ewe lamb he had bought. He raised it, and it grew up with him and his children. It shared his food, drank from his cup and even slept in his arms. It was like a daughter to him.
>
> "Now a traveler came to the rich man, but the rich man refrained from taking one of his own sheep or cattle to prepare a meal for the traveler who had come to him. Instead, he took the ewe lamb that belonged to the poor man and prepared it for the one who had come to him."
>
> David burned with anger against the man and said to Nathan, "As surely as the LORD lives, the man who did this deserves to die!"

Then Nathan said to David, "You are the man! This is what the Lord, the God of Israel says: 'I anointed you king over Israel. . . . If all this had been too little, I would have given you even more. Why did you despise the word of the LORD by doing what is evil in his eyes? You struck down Uriah the Hittite with the sword and took his wife to be your own. . . . Therefore the sword will never depart from your house, because you despised me.'" (2 Sam 12:1-10)

The story prepared David's heart to hear these strong words. Without it, the defenses he had built around his heart would have repelled the rebuke. This normally spiritually sensitive man seemed to have dulled his conscience so that he was blind to his sin. But the story burrowed right under those defenses. David finally saw the enormity of his sin, and we are privileged to have his prayer of repentance recorded for us in Psalm 51: "Have mercy on me. . . . Blot out my transgressions. . . . Against you, you only, have I sinned and done what is evil in your sight. . . . Cleanse me . . . wash me, and I will be whiter than snow" (Ps 51:1-7).

The basic evangelism story set, which is really a Bible overview, is a "must-hear" for everyone. This set reveals the gaps in a person's understanding, which helps us work out what parts of the Bible to cover in more depth. It's also a great way to get to know each other. We should quickly be able to determine the disciple's level of understanding and adapt the complexity of the story and level of discussion questions appropriately. You'll end up exploring more widely, with additional story sections, than you would with someone who doesn't have any background. Encourage disciples to be reading whole books of the Bible when they're at home to keep up with the stories: for example, Genesis, Exodus 1–20 and 32, and Luke and Acts. Especially keen readers might also read the narrative portions of Numbers and Joshua to Esther.

Storying in discipleship aims to keep challenging the "bricks" in a person's worldview. Often these bricks are not obvious. Push the discussion to greater depth, especially in the area of application. For example, you might ask, "What will happen if you ignore Jesus' command in this story?" "What could prevent you from obeying?" "How does this apply to your marriage, work or use of time? " After the basic Bible overview you have the freedom to do narratives in greater depth and to choose those that are seldom covered. It is exciting for disciples to discover life lessons from Ezra, Nehemiah, Job, various prophets and the narratives in Samuel, Kings and Chronicles.

I use the term "discipleship" to cover the whole journey from the beginning of the new life until physical death. Some cultures use the term only for the beginning stages and use other terms like "mentoring" or "coaching" for more advanced stages of the Christian journey. I would argue that we are always disciples of Jesus and therefore always need to be discipled, even if the methods change as we progress in maturity. In fact, storying has a distinct advantage when used with disciples who have been learning from the Bible for years. It's sometimes easy for them to become bored and to think, "I've heard all this before. Not Jesus calming the storm again!" But storying can open our minds and imaginations anew.

A group of missionaries was being trained to use storying in the context of small group Bible study. The training consisted of actually doing the Bible study as though they were members of a group. I chose the story of Jairus's daughter and the woman who had been bleeding for twelve years (Mk 5:21-43) to demonstrate that storying lets us revisit familiar stories and see them in a new way. The participants were amazed at the new insights they gained and how they engaged emotionally with the story. We considered how impatient Jairus must have felt as Jesus delayed to talk to the woman in the crowd. In the end he obtained far more than he requested—the raising of his daughter from the dead, not just her healing. We thought how terrified the woman must have been. She'd hoped to sneak in and gain healing and then leave before she was noticed. Jesus had a broader agenda and wanted to heal her more than just physically. We thought about our own lives and ministries, how we're often impatient for Jesus to work when he is determined to give us more than we ask for.

Storying is also a way to cover topics such as parenting, marriage, prayer, worship and repentance. Andy Smith, an American OMF missionary in the Philippines, has facilitated two-day workshops with large groups of disciples. Each workshop introduces a set of stories on a given subject. The first addresses worship, the second prayer—both important subjects for new believers. He lists all the stories that teach about these subjects. Then he chooses the twenty that portray the widest range of principles and practices on the subject. The group learns each story and then reflects on it. They distill the principles and practices that please God and those that do not. By the end of the two days, the stories have greatly reshaped participants' understanding of the subject. At the end of the workshop on worship, they have a time of worship in which they do what they've learned. At several points during the one on prayer, they stop to pray based on the lessons learned so far.

Andy noticed that one group had a shallow understanding of repentance. So he led them in looking at fourteen passages, most of which were stories. After each passage, the group wrote the answers to the following questions on a chart:

1. What sin is mentioned?

2. What command or teaching about repentance is mentioned?

3. What people are mentioned in the story?

4. What evidence is there that they repented or refused to repent?

Then the group discussed what they had observed from the story. After the final passage, each person was asked to apply the teaching by answering these four questions:

1. How would you now define or explain repentance?

2. List the things that demonstrate that someone has truly repented.

3. List the fruit of repentance that should be seen in a person's life.

4. List five specific things you'll do to apply what you've learned.[1]

Using storytelling in discipleship also helps train disciples to use storytelling with their friends. We might tell and discuss a story one week and then train it the following week. Thus disciples are not just growing in their Bible knowledge and applying it in their life but are learning how to do evangelism as well. They're also receiving a model of how to disciple. Let your group know that that the way they're being discipled is a model they can follow with others. This instills as early as possible the idea that what they learn they can and should pass on.

Storying with Bible Study Groups

Avery Willis, an author and International Missions Board missionary and executive, was a passionate proponent of Bible storying. "God wired us for stories," he said. "We like stories. We remember stories. They penetrate beyond our heads and get down into our hearts." Willis insisted that American culture was becoming more oral in its learning style and that the church was going to be left behind. One group in Idaho began to be influenced by his enthusiasm. They decided to try Bible storying in a few small groups. The experiment was so successful that they trained all their pastors, community pastors and small group leaders to use Bible storytelling. Some were reluctant at first, but they soon found that Bible storying helped all attendees learn the Bible at a greater depth than they had with other methods they'd used. Parents learned to disciple their children. Small group relationships became more real and transparent. Group members were better equipped for ministry, and leaders began to understand the spiritual needs of those they were discipling. The church also discovered that it was easier to recruit small group leaders because the method was simpler and more fun for leaders to use.[2]

I have recently begun experimenting with storying in Bible study groups. This method is completely different from the models I used previously: either working through a booklet with prepared questions or formulating discussion questions based on the style of the passage being studied.[3] But I am quickly becoming convinced of the effectiveness of storying in Bible study groups. The approach below can be used with both believers and nonbelievers if the nonbelievers are ready for discussion. First, let me describe three groups. One is a mixture of Christians and seekers, the second is a group of less mature Christians, and the third is a group of mature Christians.

Group 1. This is Amanda's group, which we discussed in chapter 9. It includes three women and three of their children, ages ten to sixteen. The women's husbands have declined to hear the stories but know that their wives might become Christians and have encouraged them to be involved. Amanda, a new believer, opens in prayer and then tells a story from the basic set. Immediately after this we group-tell the story several times, then everyone practices the whole story in pairs. After this we have a discussion time that follows one of the two basic question sets. The first week, Amanda had a tendency to talk to the children rather than the adults, but that was corrected and the group dynamics improve each week.

This group wanted to pray together from the first week. For three weeks we prayed one- or two-sentence prayers of thanksgiving based on something we'd learned from the story. In week four we added a time of sharing, and they were encouraged to pray for each other's requests. We have also been learning songs one at a time. From the fifth week the group members have been leading the discussion using questions written on cards. One person reads the first question and leads. Then she passes the card to another volunteer, who leads the next question. We've never had a problem finding volunteers because the size of the task is manageable. It seems to give the group members a sense of security knowing what the questions will be ahead of time.

The discussion is growing in depth week by week. We just did the final Old Testament section, which covers Mount Sinai, the giving of the law and the Day of Atonement. That evening we discussed why so many stories seem to talk about a lamb. Also, is God cruel to kill people who don't obey him? And why was he so upset by the golden calf? After all, the people claimed they were worshiping the God "who brought them up out of Egypt" and not a new god (Ex 32:4-5). After seven weeks of meeting, the change in the degree of involvement is marked. It is no longer just the children who dare to ask questions.

Group 2. This is a small group in a church of 250 people. All are believers, and their ages range from twenty-four to sixty-five. Only one has participated in a Bible study before, so they were initially lacking in confidence and shy about talking. Their culture does not encourage discussion but rather listening to an "expert" who shares, like a spoken commentary. They didn't want to try anything new.

Over two years they've changed dramatically. The meetings are a mix of storying and Bible study. First we covered the basic set of stories, and since then we've alternated between Old Testament (Genesis sections, 1 Samuel, Daniel and Jonah) and New Testament (John, Acts and Philippians), with occasional returns to the basic set. I've slowly learned that their favorite discussion method is the same one the first group uses: two basic sets of questions written on cards. I thought they'd be bored by answering the same questions over and over, but the discussion on those nights is far superior to any other method I come up with. The leader chooses which set of questions to use by selecting the card with those questions on it. He or she can lead discussion without elaborate preparation. Instead preparation is almost entirely meditating on the Scripture and praying for the group members.

We've been over the entire basic set at least three times, but the group has been reluctant to make storying a natural part of life. I've spent a lot of time thinking about their motivations and building in more practice time during the sessions, and there seems to be a change of heart occurring. We've been practicing the first story over and over again until the group feels confident and natural in their telling of it. This week they've been asked to tell the story to someone each day, whether it be a child for a devotional or bedtime story, an adult at the dinner table, or a neighbor or workmate in the course of the day. Next week we will go out and tell the story in an evangelistic context during our Bible study time and then come back to debrief. They've already set up these storying opportunities in advance. This approach seems to be working.

Once the group has this whole set of stories rock solid in their minds (it's almost there now), I hope each member will start another Bible study group and use storying as the main method since it's easier to lead. This initial group was the first Bible study group in the church for at least twenty years. We want to see local lay believers leading others. The group members have already taken turns leading Acts in a storying style. Even practicing twice each, they've experienced marked improvement and confidence in leading.

Of course, large parts of the Bible aren't narrative. Andrew and Jo have experimented in Australia with a simple approach to these passages. Prayer is followed by a reading of the passage. Every group member has to come up with something that they learn from the passage or a question that they want answered. No repeated comments or questions are allowed. Less confident members rush to be first to say the "easier" things and then delight in watching others try to come up with something new.

Group 3. Dr. Sam Chan is a medical doctor and theological lecturer at Sydney (Australia) Missionary and Bible College with a Ph.D. in the theology of preaching.[4] He lectures on preaching, theology, evangelism and ethics. At his local church he leads a Bible study group with professionals who have participated in groups for years. At one point he realized that many of the group members in their thirties and forties were bored, although they tried not to admit it. Sam had had a storying Bible study approach modeled to him and decided it was worth a try. He knew that stories appealed to postmodern thinkers. So he tackled a seldom-studied narrative portion in the middle of Isaiah (chapters 36–39) about King Hezekiah and Sennacherib of Babylon. He used five questions, which participants first discussed in pairs before sharing their thoughts with the whole group.

- What impresses you most in this story?
- What don't you understand in this story?
- What do you learn about people?
- What do you learn about God?
- How will this change your life this week?

Sam reports that the change in the group was immediately obvious. They loved the story, and the place was buzzing with discussion. In the past, people would forget what they'd discussed from week to week. Now not only do they remember longer but they're noticeably more alert and participatory. Group members have demonstrated an avid interest in reading Isaiah for themselves.

The next question Sam asked himself was whether this approach would work with other groups. All lecturers at Sam's Bible college are asked to lead a mission team to churches within the state, in another state or overseas. Sam's team was sent to a town in another state. He selected a group of forty- to sixty-year-olds to experiment with. How would they respond to such a different style of Bible study? Never one to choose the easy option, Sam chose a nonnarrative passage from Isaiah 55, a prophetic oracle. Sam first told the whole section twice. Then everyone was given one verse to prepare by "storyboarding"—using cartoons or drawings as memory prompts. Group members told each other their verses in pairs. Then the whole group told the chapter in sequence from verse 1. Discussion followed the five basic questions. The group discussed animatedly for ninety minutes and

Sam had to remind them to go home because they wanted to keep talking. Many reported understanding that portion of Isaiah for the first time.

I sometimes struggle to do storying with people who've been in church a long time because I doubt they'll want to listen. I was once asked to lead a women's group in Australia. I decided to do the stories from Genesis 1–3 with them so they could catch a glimpse of my work in Taiwan as well as study the Bible. Just before I opened my mouth and for the first few minutes of the story, my mind was bombarded with these thoughts: "These people have grown up in the church. They've been hearing this story for fifty or sixty years. It's too simple. How ridiculous you'll sound!" I knew I must immediately "take these thoughts captive" (2 Cor 10:5) or I'd be immobilized by my fear of seeming ridiculous. While telling the story I concurrently reminded myself of specific Scripture verses and principles—for example, all of the Bible is "God-breathed" and "useful" (2 Tim 3:16).

That day the power of storying was again revealed. Those women were hanging on every word and bubbling over with excitement as we discussed it afterward. No special audiovisual tools were used—it was just the biblical story.

Storying in Preaching

Once Sam had used storying in Bible study groups he began to think about how the approach could be applied to preaching. He had always followed the expository method that was modeled to him. To most people he seemed "successful" as he did lots of guest preaching in churches and at conferences. His style was interesting to listen to and each point was well illustrated. However, he felt that the models he'd received didn't work so well with narrative. He also wasn't convinced he was connecting with teenagers, nonnative English speakers and those without a university background. Could a storying style make people engage with the biblical text and apply it better in to their lives? Would using a storying approach lose him the interest of the more educated?

Sam decided to try a new approach. He spent most of his preparation time learning a story and meditating on it. At the same time he thought about his audience and pondered what questions they might have when they heard the story. He chose the most relevant of these questions and arranged them as his sermon points. His sermon became a retelling of the story and then a discussion answering the questions he'd thought they'd be most curious about. So for example, his sermon on the Rich Man and Lazarus (Lk 16:19-31) had this outline:

a. Why is the rich man in hell?

b. Why is there suffering in hell?

c. How do I avoid going to hell?

An evangelistic youth talk on the parable of the workers (Mt 20:1-16) asked,

a. Why isn't this unfair?

b. Why does everyone get the same pay?

c. What is God trying to teach me?

Some of the basic discussion questions could also form sermon points. That is, you could use these three:

a. What do we learn about people?

b. What do we learn about God?

c. How does this apply to our lives this week?

At Easter, Sam and another storytelling advocate did the Bible readings in an unconventional way. Rather than reading the passages, they told stories based on John 19 on Good Friday and John 20 on Easter Sunday. Then the preacher spoke on these stories. A professional woman in her seventies with numerous degrees came up to Sam afterward and said, "That was wonderful. You could hear a pin drop. We were listening to every word." As someone who communicates for a living, Sam says he has learned to read people's eyes. He has found that his new way of preaching engages listeners far more deeply. They're not only more attentive but they're remembering the Bible and becoming enthralled by it.

In Sam's own life he has noticed that he is learning large sections of narrative and that he often finds himself mulling over the stories. Through storying he is noticing things about the stories that he'd missed in the past. Storying is taking him deeper into the Scripture. He's never been a Bible verse memorizer, but suddenly he can tell whole chapters of the Bible, both narrative and nonnarrative.

Preaching in this way requires courage because it is so different from the models most of us have received. One theological college principal admitted that he's afraid to do it too often because he fears criticism for being too simple.

I've found that when I'm asked to give a Bible talk, my approach has changed. For a start, I now nearly always choose narrative passages to speak from. Often the epistles' doctrine becomes backup for the story rather than the other way around. For example, in telling the story of the unforgiving servant (Mt 18:21-35) I can pull in teaching on forgiveness from doctrinal sections of the Bible (Eph 4:25-26; Mt 5:23-24, 38-48). I also find myself illustrating points from within the biblical narratives rather than using lots of outside illustrations. Many teaching passages have background stories that make it easier for people to identify with. For example, I explain the story of the church at Ephesus as I teach on Ephesians.

Does this mean that we avoid nonnarrative sections? At the moment my thoughts on this are untested, so I offer them tentatively. I believe we tend to think of stories as "simple" and doctrine as "meat." However, I suspect that all of the doctrines of the Bible are also contained in story form. The more we delve into the narrative sections the more we'll discover what depths they contain. However, this depth is communicated in a way that all people can digest.

Many of the psalms and epistles have story backgrounds. Sharing on these passages in the context of their stories will make them easier to remember. For example, you could teach Paul's letters in the context of the missionary journeys of Acts. Psalms like Psalm 51 make far more sense taught as part of a 2 Samuel series on King David. Some of Moses' psalms would be remembered more easily as part of a series on his life. A series on Peter would work wonderfully if it linked his life and early character with the letters he wrote when mature. This series would lead to rejoicing at the greatness of God in changing such a man and using him so mightily despite all his sin and mistakes.

Sam, with his extensive preaching opportunities, is pushing the boundaries with nonnarrative told in a storying style. When his church did a sermon series on Malachi, Sam told a story instead of reading the Bible passage. This worked, even though Malachi isn't story but prophetic oracle. The "story" of Malachi captured the dialogue between God and Israel.

A church needs balanced preaching from all sections of Scripture. Storying is not the only way to preach, and using storying exclusively would not be helpful. Congregations need to hear preaching from the Epistles, Prophets, apocalyptic sections, wisdom and poetic sections of Scripture as well as the narratives. But my experience has been that I hear most preaching from the four Gospels and the Epistles and little from the rest of the Bible. A mixture of preaching and teaching styles will engage the full range of learning styles that God has created among his people.

Storying in Theological Education

The Bible college I attended has the excellent practice of having "missionaries in residence" come and live at the college for a week at a time. They listen to lectures and have input as appropriate. As a result of experiencing this model and also being the "missionary" on numerous occasions, I like to visit other theological colleges. Recently I visited a college in a continent that has large numbers of oral learners. I was saddened to see that the lecturers taught as though they were lecturing Western university graduates. Some of the students expressed disappointment to me that the lectures weren't reaching their own hearts and certainly weren't helping them teach the Bible to their own people. When they used the model they'd experienced, their listeners found it boring and irrelevant and quickly stopped paying attention. I am grateful to the college for allowing me a short time to demonstrate storying methods. The students could immediately see the relevance to their ministries, but sadly only a few lecturers came to the session.

I would like to share a story from a courageous missionary Bible college lecturer who had the humility to see that he hadn't communicated well for many years and the courage to change:

> After six years of church planting in central Thailand, I was asked to teach at the Bangkok Bible College, a career that spanned the next sixteen years as I progressed from academic dean to seminary dean and eventually founding director of a new seminary. During those years I taught as I had been taught in seminary. I simply transferred a Western template of pedagogy to the Thai classroom and fulfilled the expectation of the "enlightened" expert, using almost exclusively a propositional style of lecturing. My compliant Thai students conformed to this style, thinking that highly literate missionaries from the West must surely have the most effective ways of teaching theology. Added to this were the accreditation requirements that forced the school to conform to Western content and curriculum.
>
> I probably would have finished out my teaching career in the same mode, if it were not for the qualitative research I did on my PhD coupled with exposure to the field of orality. My studies revealed that at their core the Thai are actually oral learners and although they are functionally literate, their preference is to receive information in a oral/aural

mode. My paradigm shift to live Bible storytelling (rather than analytical, logical and propositional teaching) has resonated with the Thai, and I am now having numerous chances to prove the oral nature of the Thai through story seminars taught by a team of Thai and myself in both urban and rural contexts.

Years ago, a senior worker in my mission agency tried to sway my thinking toward orality when he told me, "Larry, the Thai are not readers; they learn orally and relationally." With so much invested in a literate bias along with my Western expositional tools, I found this assertion hard to swallow. However, during the past few years of teaching the seventy-five percent of the Bible that is narrative with an oral/story approach, I have seen transformational changes in the lives of Thai that I never saw during the previous quarter-century of work.

For instance, my propositional exegesis of the Bartimaeus story no doubt evoked a cognitive response to the truths of that story on the part of my hearers. But now, after helping my audience identify deeply with this blind beggar, they seem to respond not just with their minds, but also their heart and gut as well. "What can I do for you?" no longer becomes a question for an ancient character in the Bible but hits home through a direct application to people's felt needs. Exegetical tools are still important to me, but mainly in the area of background preparation of stories. The oral tool, which I overlooked in the past, has surprisingly become one of the most powerful tools on my communication belt.[5]

After interviewing Sam Chan about his use of storying in Bible study groups and preaching, I challenged him to think about how to use it in his lecturing with predominantly highly educated Westerners. He took up the challenge and was willing to share two of his first attempts. His theology of creation lecture gave him an opportunity. He had seventy students (bachelor's and master's levels) for three hours. First he told the story of Genesis 1. Then he divided the class into pairs and they discussed two questions: "What impressed you about the story?" and "What questions do you have of the story?" They then shared their responses with the whole group. Sam demonstrated how many of their questions were answered in theology, convincing the students of the relevance of the course. In his second and third hours he covered the theology of creation, making sure he answered as many of their questions as possible.

Sam noticed that this year his students were noticeably more enthusiastic about theology. He comments, "Typically, in theology, we teach the subject in a low-context method. That is, we begin with the theory and then end with the concrete application. But by beginning with the Bible stories, we begin with the concrete application and now try to generate the theory. This is the high-context method. The high-context method means that students see the relevance of theology to their lives both spiritually and practically. It makes them want to turn up and they come with expectations of learning something useful."

In his evangelism classes, Sam is now teaching storytelling as one of the basic ways of evangelizing the West, most of whom he believes "can be classified as postliterate oral learners." He teaches his students stories they can immediately go out and use in their own evangelism.[6]

Reflection

1. What has been applicable in this chapter to your situation?

2. Do you disagree with anything that was said? Work out a way to test whether your beliefs are correct.

3. What has surprised or challenged you?

4. Take time to brainstorm ideas for changing your communication.

5. Try one idea from this chapter and evaluate what you learned. Share this experience with someone else. Consider forming an accountability or learning partnership with someone.

Epilogue

I have been in my current town of service for two and a half years. By the world's standards I have had little success, seeing only a few new believers come to faith. Thankfully God judges success differently. I look to the harvest to come because many people have heard at least fourteen sections of the Bible. Believers in the area are slowly becoming inspired to do storying outside their church buildings. They're taking the stories into their neighborhoods and homes. The day will come when the flame of the gospel will ignite families' lives and spread the light into this dark place.

You might feel daunted at the magnitude of the task in front of you. Don't let fear stop you. Just take one step at a time. Learn one story and start telling that. If it doesn't seem to go well the first time, don't give up. Consider why you met with a negative response. Usually it is just a small thing that needs adjusting. Pray and ask the Holy Spirit to show you how to proceed. You might be surprised at how he leads you.

Two months ago I was convicted to try to meet some local community leaders one by one and ask them about their area of town and the issues they faced. I was also praying that God might lead me to people of influence who would not only want to hear stories themselves but be bridges to reach other people.

The third set of community leaders that I interviewed, Mr. and Mrs. Tan, had three other visitors when I showed up, another couple and a grandmother. I hadn't intended to share any stories on my first visit, but one of the men asked me to once he heard me say I was a storyteller.

I told the creation story, and I was thrilled when they asked me to come back the following week. The next Monday it was pouring rain, so I had low expectations that anyone would come. Imagine my surprise when I found all five waiting for me. I have now told ten stories, one each week. This group doesn't discuss readily, but with each week interaction improves. I'm praying that one day these five become believers and that this group transitions naturally into a house church.

Just as this book was being completed, four people decided to follow Jesus. Amanda's storying group has two new believers, and the others are getting closer. Another lady has just been baptized and is rejoicing in new life after hearing two and a half years of stories. Mr. Lee in the bicycle shop has also decided to follow Jesus after about eighteen months of stories.

Sam, James, Larry, Amanda and many others have found that storying takes us on a journey of discovery. Not only do we learn to communicate with a wider range of people and at a deeper level, but we delve deeper into Scripture ourselves. Our listeners appreciate our evangelism style. When we talk with them, discussion is animated as we all share what we're learning. We hope that you will join us in sharing the greatest story of them all.

I will probably never meet most of you until the final day. I look forward to hearing your testimonies of how God used you to tell his salvation story to others.

APPENDIX A
Extra Discussion Questions

When you hold discussion sessions, you could just ask the two basic sets of questions each time and have excellent discussions. Asking the same questions over and over gives some people a sense of security and eases their fears because they know what's coming. But others might become bored. In that case, you'll want to branch out in your questions and discussion topics. First, here's a reminder of the basic questions:

Set 1

1. What do you like best about this story? Why?

2. What do you struggle with or not understand?

3. What do you learn about people?

4. What do you learn about God?

5. What needs to change in your life after hearing this story? (Alternate wording: If this story is true, what do you need to change in your life?)

Set 2

1. What truths do you see in this story?

2. Which truth most impacts you?

3. How could this truth impact your life?

4. Who else needs to hear this story?

Following are some additional discussion questions for each story that I've used at various times. You'll need to work out whether they're suitable for your situation. Even if they're not, hopefully they'll stimulate your thinking.

Creation (Gen 1–2)

1. Why did God rest? Was he tired?

2. Based on the story of the creation of Eve—especially the part about how the man "must leave his father and mother"—what is God's plan for marriage and why did he create it?

3. How are people different from animals? What are the implications for being made in the image of God? How do male and female together reflect that image?

Rebellion (Gen 3)

1. What was the snake's purpose? What methods did he use with Adam and Eve?

2. What do you think the word "sin" means? What does the Bible teach about sin in this story?

3. What were the results of our rebellion against God?

4. If God knew we'd use our freedom to rebel against him, why did he give us freedom?

Noah (Gen 6–9)

1. What are the two ways to live mentioned in this story? What were the results of those choices?

2. Is the majority always right? How easy is it to be in the minority?

3. What sorts of things would make it worthwhile to be in the minority?

4. What could encourage you to keep going if all your friends were laughing at you?

5. Noah was called a "righteous man." What do you think this means? (Ask before and after telling the story. Be sure to emphasize that it does not mean Noah was perfect. Clue—Gen 6:9.)

Abraham (Gen 12:1–25:11)

1. Why do you think Abraham didn't trust God regarding God's promise of giving Abraham and his wife a son (Gen 15)?

2. What would you struggle to trust God with?

3. How do you think Abraham felt when God asked him to sacrifice his son (Gen 22)?

4. Why do you think he trusted God that time?

Exodus (Ex 1–12)

1. Why do you think God allowed the Israelites to suffer in slavery?

2. Why do you think God sent ten plagues? Didn't he have the power to achieve the Israelites' freedom with one huge plague?

3. What could the Israelites have learned from the ten plagues? The Egyptians?

4. If your family were in Egypt at the time, how many males in your family could have died?

5. How would you have felt if you heard about the way to save them? What would you have done?

Sinai, Tabernacle (Ex 19–20:21; 32; Lev 16)

1. Why do you think God chose to use festivals and the tabernacle to teach about himself?

2. What did these things teach?

3. What do we learn about people through Israel's history to this point?

4. What do we learn about God?

Jesus' Birth (Mt 1–2; Lk 1–2)

1. If you were arranging for the arrival of the creator, how would you have arranged it? What kind of family and situation would you have chosen?

2. What do we learn about God from how he arranged it?

3. Why do you think the visitors from the east gave those three gifts?

4. Jesus fulfilled all the hundreds of Old Testament prophecies. What do we learn about God from the fulfilling of the prophecies?

Jesus' Ministry

The specific questions you ask will depend on which stories you choose.

1. Why might Jesus have done this miracle?

2. What were the various responses to the miracle? Why did people respond that way?

3. What might each of the observers have learned from this situation?

Jesus' Death

1. Did Jesus have the power to save himself from the cross? Why did he not choose to do so?

2. What do you think the people of Jesus' day would have thought when the sky was dark from midday to 3 p.m. (Lk 23:44)?

3. Why did the temple curtain split from top to bottom (Lk 23:45)?

4. What do we learn from Peter's story (Lk 22:31-34, 54-62)?

Jesus' Resurrection and Ascension

1. What evidence is there for the resurrection? (Don't rush this question.)

2. What if Jesus hadn't risen from the dead? Is Jesus' resurrection essential to Christian faith?

3. If Jesus did rise from the dead, how would that change the world?

4. What did Jesus' last command mean? Think about each section (Acts 1:8).

5. Why might the disciples have kept gazing at the sky (Acts 1:11)?

6. Does it make a difference that Jesus came to earth and lived and died?

7. If Jesus will return to judge everyone, how should that affect our daily lives?

APPENDIX B
Different Storying Methods

During the time I was learning to use storying myself, I noticed that there were various schools of thought about it. I will try to simplify what I've noticed and not misrepresent the basics.

Chronological Bible Storying

The first method I encountered was chronological Bible storying. This kind of storying often starts with the creation and rebellion of a portion of the spiritual beings. This introduction initially seemed to me to suit the Taiwanese worldview. It was helpful to discuss where evil spirits ("ghosts," in their terminology) came from.

When I first started storying I followed the model I was given and started with the spiritual creatures' rebellion. I was always very careful with the story, as it does not exist as a discrete story in Scripture and there is some controversy surrounding it. When I used it (which was for several years), I included only these basic points: Satan was once an angel. At some point he became proud and led a minority of the angels in rebellion against God. For that he was banished from heaven and now works in opposition to God.

I kept using this story despite some misgivings because it was an easy way to introduce the stories in a culture that believes in evil spirits and fears them. It made sense to start where the listeners were. In addition, I didn't agree with those who took exception to the interpretation of Ezekiel 28:12-17 and Isaiah 14. Those people point out (correctly) that these passages are prophecies to Tyre and Babylon—that they do not, in fact, tell us the story of Satan and his fall. However, if you look carefully at the prophecies, you see some curious things. The Tyre prophecy talks of a "guardian cherub" who was present in Eden (Ezek 28:13-14), with the description, "You were blameless . . . from the day you were created till wickedness was found in you" (Ezek 28:15). This guardian cherub was then thrown out of God's "mountain," presumably where God lived. I cannot see how these verses apply to Tyre or its king. He was not in existence that early and he certainly was never created blameless. Like us, he would have been born infected by sin. I believe that in this prophecy Satan is the "type" of all pride and rebellion, and anyone who behaves like him is equated to him.

The Isaiah 14 passage is similar. This Scripture describes someone called "O morning star, son of the dawn" (Is 14:12). This being becomes proud and wants to be like God himself (Is 14:12-14) and so is humbled into the grave and the depths of the pit (Is 14:15). Yes, this is what eventually happened to Babylon, but the sense of the passage is that it's talking about something that happened long ago and that anyone who sets himself up against God is following Satan's pattern. Genesis 3 presents the exact same temptation—the desire to "be like God" (Gen 3:5). Thus, all who follow this pattern are fulfilling their "father" Satan's type.

However, I did eventually stop telling this story at the beginning of my set. Here are my reasons:

1. The Bible doesn't do it. If God decided to start his Word off with Genesis 1, it is very likely the best place to start.

2. I didn't want to give Satan too prominent a place. I wanted the Savior in the center of the story. Satan doesn't deserve any glory. It's interesting to note in reading the Bible how seldom he is

mentioned. He is certainly not the "equal but opposite" figure that is so beloved in Taoist and other philosophies.

3. There are more natural places to talk about Satan and his purposes and methods—for example, when telling the story of Genesis 3. Another place is after the initial story set when I tell the story of Jesus' temptations in the desert. Quite often I will return to the Genesis 3 story and highlight Satan's methods and purpose and bring in a few extra verses like 2 Corinthians 11:14 or 1 Peter 5:8. Sometimes I will then share the story of the likely origins of Satan and the demons. Normally when I tell the story of Jesus' authority over demons, someone will ask a question that allows discussion about Satan to come up naturally.

Since chopping out that story and choosing to start exactly where the Bible does, I haven't noticed any lesser understanding from my listeners. Sometimes they will ask a question during discussion that allows me to tell this story. My basic story set is a chronological telling of the salvation story and owes much to this approach.

Memorized Bible Stories

I still haven't heard this approach in person, but it has been presented to me as only way to ensure that the storyteller doesn't skew the Bible. As I've said to the advocates of this method I've encountered, "We interpret with the very tone of our voice and the Bible stories we choose." Even pauses insert interpretation. I don't think memorizing the story protects us from heresy. If someone is intent on using the Bible for his or her own ends, no method will protect them. The only protections we have are persistent prayer and a humble attitude that allows anyone to question and correct us. I've found that to be a tremendous protection.

The problem with memorized stories is that there is simply a limit to our ability to memorize. Also, it requires so much work that many potential storytellers will be put off from attempting it.

Bible Telling

This is the term John Walsh uses to describe what he does. He seeks to be accurate in his storytelling and is careful about embellishing his stories. Many of his stories can be heard at www.bible telling.org. This style is one that I have found to be biblically accurate and easy for people to reproduce. It requires no fancy materials and encourages people to read the Bible. The style I use is basically Bible telling with a chronological order added in my first story set.

In the end, it doesn't matter what we label our story style. The questions to ask are these: Is it true to the Bible? Is it Christ-focused? Is it reproducible by those we work with, or is our style too complicated?

APPENDIX C
Training Checklist

Before you begin to train a person or group in storying, it's helpful to think through your answers to these questions:

1. What is your purpose for this person or group?

2. How long will the training go on for?

3. Who are the trainees?

4. Are some of them illiterate or functionally illiterate?

5. Have they ever been trained in evangelism? What topics were covered? Are they using what they learned?

6. What are the "bricks" in their worldview regarding evangelism and storying? That is, what misconceptions do they have?

7. Do you need to train some basic evangelism principles? Which ones?

8. What are their needs in terms of storying?

9. How many stories are you hoping to train? Which ones and why?

10. How many will come to the training sessions? Will you limit numbers?

11. What is the training area like in size? Lighting? Are there other areas available so you can spread out at times?

12. How will you arrange seating?

13. What kinds of presentation methods will you use?

Appendix D
Sample Stories

I have deliberately chosen not to place transcripts of whole stories in this book. Written stories simply do not communicate in the same way oral stories do. Rather, I have recorded stories and posted them at <storyingthescriptures.com>. You can listen to the entire set of basic stories in English or Mandarin Chinese. There are also training notes listed in the comments section under each video. The Mandarin stories have been prepared for those unfamiliar with the Bible. They include introductions and conclusions to help listeners' understanding grow.

There are also six stories on Daniel (in English) and short training videos on preparing a story from the biblical text and learning the creation story (as a model for how to learn a story). Over time more stories and training videos may be added.

This site also includes a forum so that you can ask questions and discuss with other storytellers online. Please submit accounts of how you've used storying in your context to encourage others.

John Walsh's website also has many sample stories: <bible telling.org>.

Acknowledgments

This book was a team effort. First I would like to thank my faithful prayer supporters. Your "knee time" has been a major factor in keeping me in Taiwan. Maybe one day we will learn how much of the entire work was actually done by the pray-ers. Thank you to those who suggested I write this book and who prayed with me through the long process. Many times I wanted to give up, but your spurred me on. Anybody would be blessed to have such a team.

Thank you to Lindsay Brown who met me at a student conference in Australia in 2008. Your interest in a stranger resulted in your asking to hear a story. You then put my name forward to lead a storying workshop at the Lausanne Congress of Cape Town 2010. The title of the workshop prompted me to write a book to match it.

Miriam Adeney led a writers' workshop in Hong Kong in 2010 and helped me craft the first draft of this book. She encouraged me to seek a publisher at a time when I wanted to give up.

Many people have read the manuscript and offered comments, some encouragements and others perceptive critiques that weren't always easy to swallow. Thanks for having the courage. Thank you to the two readers on behalf of IVP. I hope it is obvious that I listened to your comments and that they shaped the book. Any remaining errors and unpolished parts are my responsibility. I was particularly encouraged by those who immediately went out and started to implement parts of what they'd read. This book is achieving its purpose only when it is put into practice. I dream of huge numbers of people storytelling in their cultural contexts.

Thank you to John Walsh for coming to Taiwan in 2009. You've become a storying mentor and have always promptly answered my many questions.

Thank you to Fiona Collison, Judy Dillon and Lesley Hicks, other prayer partners, for helping me with grammar. Thanks to Lesley for encouraging me with stories of your writing, editing and publishing experiences.

Thank you to those who have shared their stories with me, asked questions that made me think and discussed storying with me: Andy Smith, John G., Andrew and Joanna Wong, Rob and Donna, Jeff and Bethany, Maria, Richard C., Angie P., Julie Irving, Ruth France, Steve McKerney, Bronwyn, Sin Ee, Steve and Shannon (via Skype—we've never met personally), Harold, Adrian Cerbu and Golden Orchid, Amanda and Ivy in Taiwan. Thanks too to Sam Chan and Larry Dinkins for sharing some of your stories. Learning to story is a humbling adventure.

Ansonia Wong spent two days video recording and teaching someone technologically challenged how to edit all the videos in preparation for the website. Golden Orchid and Sharon Tsai helped me prepare the Mandarin videos, one by telling stories and the other by assisting with the written opening and closing comments on each video. Kath Henderson helped with all the other aspects of the website. What a team!

Thank you to OMF. I feel privileged to belong to this family. We have leaders who dare to try new things and who are humble learners. I am excited about the future as we learn more about communicating gospel truth in the best way possible for each culture.

Thank you too to IVP/USA for taking a risk on an unknown Australian. Al Hsu, my editor, has been an encouragement from day one. You gave me plenty of critique but you said it oh so graciously. My publishing experience with the whole team has been excellent. You're an efficient team that treats your authors like family. May you continue to bring Jesus much glory.

Lastly, grateful thanks to all those who allowed me to try stories on them. Especially those early listeners who endured stories as yet unpracticed. And to the many people I've met on planes, trains and buses, I know that our meetings were orchestrated by the orchestrator of all things. I am confidently expecting to meet you on the last day. It will be wonderful to hear the full story of God's grace to you.

Notes

Introduction

[1]OMF International was started by Hudson Taylor in 1865 as the China Inland Mission. It now works with East Asians worldwide, both in East Asia but also with the "Asian diaspora"—those scattered through the world for work or study. More information is at <www.omf.org>.

Chapter 1: Why Storying?

[1]For example, Antoine Rutayisire of Rwanda asked how the genocide of 1994 was possible in a country in which such a high proportion of people claimed to be Christians. One major reason he gave was poor discipleship, which meant that the Bible wasn't applied to people's lives. Thus they saw nothing incongruous between murdering their neighbors and claiming to follow Jesus. Antoine Rutayisire, "Building the Peace of Christ in our Divided and Broken World," Lausanne Conference Plenary Session 2, October 19, 2010.

[2]Kendall F. Haven, *Story Proof: The Science Behind the Startling Power of Story* (Westport, Conn.: Libraries Unlimited, 2007), pp. 15-17.

[3]Ibid., p. 99.

[4]Ibid., p. 87.

[5]Ibid., p. 67.

[6]Ibid., pp. 4, 7.

[7]Three main kinds of learners have been identified: visual (learn by seeing, including reading), auditory (through hearing) and kinesthetic (by actually doing). For an excellent explanation of this see chapter two, "Helping People Learn," in Karen and Rod Morris, *Leading Better Bible Studies* (Sydney, Australia: Aquila, 1997), pp. 17-44. Many evangelistic and teaching methods only cater to one or two of the learning styles. Storying

appeals to all learning styles, especially when one of the more active ways of applying the stories is used (see pp. 141-43).

[8]Don Carson, *The Gagging of God* (Grand Rapids: Zondervan, 1996), pp. 501-4.

[9]Daniel Sanchez, J. O. Terry, and LaNette W. Thompson, *Bible Storying for Church Planting* (Fort Worth, Tex.: Church Starting Network, 2008), p. xiv.

[10]Mark Snowden, "Orality: The Next Wave of Mission Advance," *Mission Frontiers* (January-February 2004) <www.missionfrontiers.org/issue/article/orality-the-next-wave-of-mission-advance>.

[11]Rick Richardson, *Re-imagining Evangelism: Inviting Friends on a Spiritual Journey* (Downers Grove, Ill.: InterVarsity Press, 2006), pp. 84-87. Richardson also notes the importance of personal story/testimony. Testimonies are particularly helpful either to intrigue people to hear more or to support the biblical story and show its relevance to modern life. They do not replace the need to hear the biblical story.

[12]The "links in the chain" and "brick wall" diagrams in this chapter can be found in Christine Dillon, *1-2-1 Discipleship: Helping One Another Grow Spiritually* (Fearn, U.K.: Christian Focus, 2009). These diagrams have been major influences on my thinking about evangelism and discipleship.

[13]Miriam Adeney, "Communication and Continuity Through Oral Transmission" in *Communicating Christ Through Story and Song: Orality in Buddhist Contexts*, ed. Paul H. De Neui (Pasedena, Calif.: William Carey Library, 2008), p. 88.

[14]Kevin M. Bradt, *Story as a Way of Knowing* (Kansas City, Mo.: Sheed & Ward, 1997), p. 199.

[15]Walter Ong, *Orality and Literacy* (New York: Methuen, 1982), pp. 69, 74.

[16]Haven, *Story Proof*, p. 111.

[17]David Eastwood, from his OMF seminar "Changing Worldviews: The Power of Story" given in Hengchun, Taiwan, on March 1, 2008.

[18]Tom Wright, *The New Testament and the People of God* (Minneapolis: Fortress, 1992), p. 38.

[19]John Walsh, "Chiang Mai," *Story Times Journal*, Florida Storytellers Association (summer 2011) <flstory.org/storytimes-journal/>.

Chapter 2: Learning from Biblical Models

[1]David Eastwood, from his OMF seminar "Changing Worldviews: The Power of Story," given in Hengchun, Taiwan, March 1, 2008.

Chapter 3: Choosing Suitable Stories

[1]Daniel Sanchez, J. O. Terry, and LaNette W. Thompson, *Bible Storying for Church Planting* (Fort Worth, Tex.: Church Starting Network, 2008), pp. 76-77.

[2]The Reeds' story can be found in more detail in Barbara Flory Reed, *Beyond the Great Darkness: Modern Missionary Pioneering in the Jungles of the Philippines* (Singapore: OMF Books, 1987).

[3]These African proverbs were found at <www.afriprov.org>.

[4]J. O. Terry, *Basic Bible Storying: Preparing and Presenting Bible Stories for Evangelism, Discipleship, Training and Ministry* (Fort Worth, Tex.: Church Starting Network, 2006), p. 51.

[5]This idea came from a course by Michael Bennett, author of *Christianity Explained* (Brisbane, Australia: Scripture Union, 1985). I have regularly used Bennett's chapter on Jesus' authority as the basis of children's ministry camps and now in storying.

Chapter 4: Preparing Stories from the Biblical Text

[1]John Walsh, personal email, June 29, 2010. I am indebted to Walsh, an American storyteller, whose training session I attended in Taiwan in July 2009. He has graciously answered many questions via email. He has written several books on storytelling, and you can listen to his stories at <www.bibletelling.org>.

[2]Walter Ong, *Orality and Literacy* (New York: Methuen, 1982), p. 59.

[3]Ibid., p. 68.

[4]Dale Jones, "Moving Towards Oral Communication of the Gospel: Experiences from Cambodia," in *Communicating Christ Through Story and Song: Orality in Buddhist Contexts*, ed. Paul H. De Neui (Pasedena, Calif.: William Carey Library, 2008), pp. 190-91.

[5]Martin Goldsmith, personal conversation, Taichung, Taiwan, July 1, 2010.

[6]For further insight on this topic, see Michael Novelli, *Shaped by the Story* (Grand Rapids: Zondervan, 2008).

[7]Retired OMF missionary Martin Goldsmith has extensive experience within Jewish, Islamic and British contexts.

Chapter 5: Getting Started

[1]A Campus Crusade project, the *Jesus* film has been dubbed in many languages, including some that haven't yet received the Bible in their language. The organization has now added a storying introduction that includes the stories of creation, Abraham and others to prepare the way for the Luke story. It can be watched online in more than 1000 languages at <www.jesusfilm.org/film-and-media/watch-the-film>.

[2]J. O. Terry, *Basic Bible Storying: Preparing and Presenting Bible Stories for Evangelism, Discipleship, Training and Ministry* (Fort Worth, Tex.: Church Starting Network, 2006).

Chapter 6: Leading Discussion

[1]These questions come from John Walsh, who tells me that his storying approach was developed with his close friend Mark Getz. See his website to listen to story samples: <www.bibletelling.org>.

[2]J. O. Terry, *Basic Bible Storying: Preparing and Presenting Bible Stories for Evangelism, Discipleship, Training and Ministry* (Fort Worth, Tex.: Church Starting Network, 2006), p. 102.

[3]Kevin M. Bradt, *Story as a Way of Knowing* (Kansas City, Mo.: Sheed & Ward, 1997), p. 52. Bradt has some worthwhile things to say about Bible storytelling and how he started (his sermons were boring his listeners). However, I do not endorse his style of storytelling in the samples he gives as part of the books, mostly because I prefer stories that are told as closely as possible to the biblical text and don't contain speculative thoughts.

[4]Ibid, p. 159.

[5]Ibid, p. 164.

[6]Ibid, p. 104.

[7]Terry, *Basic Bible Storying*, pp. 96-97.

Chapter 7: Discussion Dynamics

[1]The set I use is in Chinese and might also be available in Japanese as its author was a Japanese pastor. There are volumes on Genesis, Moses and Joshua, David and Solomon, Jesus' life, parables and Acts. Available through Christian Communications Inc. USA, 9600 Bellaire Blvd., Houston, TX 77036, (713) 778-1144.

[2]For more information on solar-powered or hand-wound MP3 players see <www.megavoice.com>. For battery-powered options see <www.my-ibible .com/products.html>.

Chapter 8: The Basics

[1]See this site for one idea: <www.storyrunners.com>.

[2]John Walsh, "Storying Training" held in Taichung, Taiwan, July 13-17, 2009.

[3]Miriam Adeney, *Daughters of Islam: Building Bridges with Muslim Women* (Downers Grove, Ill.: InterVarsity Press, 2002), pp. 162-66.

[4]Personal email, July 27, 2011. This and other ideas are contributed by my friend J. G. and used with permission. J. G.'s name is withheld for security reasons as he works in a creative access nation.

Chapter 9: Motivating Trainers

[1]The site <storyingthescriptures.com> has been set up to allow you to listen to sample stories in English and Mandarin. There are also links to other

storying sites and a forum for asking questions and sharing your experiences wth storying for the encouragement of others.
[2]David McClelland, *Human Motivation* (Cambridge: Cambridge University Press, 1987).
[3]See <simplythestory.org/oralbiblestories>. While this website gives the impression that storying is only for oral learners, I believe everyone will love storying.
[4]John Walsh, "Storying Training" held in Taichung, Taiwan, July 13-17, 2009.
[5]John Walsh, personal email, August 21, 2011.

Chapter 10: Evangelistic Storying with Different Audiences
[1]A wide range of excellent resources is available to help us understand Islam, both for those of us who encounter Muslims in a Western context and for those living in Muslim areas. Some that I have found helpful include Miriam Adeney, *Daughters of Islam: Building Bridges with Muslim Women* (Downers Grove, Ill.: InterVarsity Press, 2002); Colin Chapman, *Cross and Crescent: Responding to the Challenge of Islam* (Downers Grove, Ill.: InterVarsity Press, 2007); Bill A. Musk, *The Unseen Face of Islam* (Crowborough, U.K.: Monarch, 1989) (Musk's book is particularly useful for understanding the underlying animism in much of Islam); Bilquis Sheikh, *I Dared to Call Him Father* (Eastbourne, U.K.: Kingsway, 1978) (the author, who came to Christ from a Muslim background, highlights many Muslim misunderstandings about the gospel and also the challenges of conversion to Christianity).
[2]Ray Galea, *Nothing in my Hand I Bring: Understanding the Differences between Roman Catholic and Protestant Beliefs* (Kingsford, Australia: Matthias Media, 2007). This book, written by a former Roman Catholic of Maltese background, is gentle and sensitive. Galea's testimony reveals his previous beliefs and how God led him on a journey to understand the gospel more fully.
[3]Martin Goldsmith and Rosemary Harley, *Who Is My Neighbour?* (Milton Keynes, U.K.: Authentic Media/OMF, 2002). This is a good book for general understanding of other religions and new religious movements. It is written for a Western context by experienced missionaries and practitioners who recognize that many Westerners meet and work with those from many religious backgrounds. Also helpful is Larry A. Nichols, George Mather, and Alvin J. Schmidt, *Encyclopedic Dictionary of Cults, Sects, and World Religions* (Grand Rapids: Zondervan, 2006).
[4]I used an Australian resource called "Two Ways to Live"; see <www.matthiasmedia.com.au/2wtl>. Some other suggestions include the "gospel

bridge," <findinggrace.com/gospel/bridge.htm>, and the "evangecube," <simplysharejesus.com>. I find it helpful to use a replacement phrase like "rebellion against God" or "claiming to be the center of the universe" instead of sin. Although these illustrations have the advantage of being visual they are still communicating abstract propositions. I believe they could be adapted and told as a story.

[5]David Murrow, *Why Men Hate Going to Church* (Nashville: Thomas Nelson, 2004). Also, the website <churchformen.com> contains excellent resources and issues to think through in reaching, teaching and training men.

Chapter 11: Storying for Christian Teaching

[1]Andy Smith, personal emails and conversations, 2011. The fourteen passages Smith used for the repentance series were Gen 35:1-7; Lev 6:1-7; Is 30:8-18; Jer 36:1-24; Hos 14:1-4; Mt 21:28-32; 27:3-5; Lk 3:2-14; 19:1-10; Acts 16:22-34; 19:17-20; Rev 2:4-5; 3:15-20; 9:19-20. The order is variable.

[2]L. Sells, "Avery Willis' Last Dream," *Mission Frontiers* (January 2011) <www.missionfrontiers.org/issue/article/avery-willis-last-dream>.

[3]Karen and Rod Morris, *Leading Better Bible Studies: Essential Skills for Effective Small Groups* (Sydney, Australia: Aquila, 1997). Before I started using storying in Bible study groups, this was the best book I'd read on leading Bible studies. It contains plentiful hints on leading Bible study groups, plus research on learning styles and teaching.

[4]Series of personal emails and Skype interviews with Sam Chan, July 2011.

[5]Personal email from Larry Dinkins, December 21, 2010.

[6]Personal email correspondence with Sam Chan, August 2011.